# PRAYER AT WORK

# PRAYER AT WORK

*Take Faith to Work*
*and Put Faith to Work*

Ann Bamford Adams, D. Min.

Chapel Place Press
Wellesley Hills, Massachusetts

The verse quoted on page 131 is taken from "Bring Many Names" by Brian Wren (c) 1989 Hope Publishing Co., Carol Stream, IL 60188. All rights reserved. Used by permission.

The quotation on page 169—170 is from the article "It Starts with Uncertainty," *Shambala Sun*, November 1999, by Margaret Wheatley and Pema Chodron. Published on the website of Margaret Wheatley, www.margaretwheatley.com. Used by permission.

The quotation on page 211 from Scott Senau is from *Quotes for the Journey/Wisdom* for the Way compiled by Gordon S. Jackson. Published by Navpress. Used by permission.

All biblical quotations are from the New Revised Standard Version Bible, copyright 1989, Division of Christian Education of the National Council of the Churches of Christ in the United States of America. Used by permission. All rights reserved.

Cover design by William Murphy

Cover photo by Erica Johnson

ISBN 0-9745123-0-3

Library of Congress Control Number: 2003096333

To the members and staff
of the Wellesley Hills Congregational Church,
United Church of Christ,
who taught me how to pray

and to
Carolyn Shaw Bell
who has always believed in me

## ACKNOWLEDGEMENTS

Numerous people helped me in the creation of this book. Many friends and readers of my weekly prayers encouraged me to go ahead and publish these prayers. The Friday After Ours gang consistently supported my labors.

Bruce Dishman patiently taught me the rudiments of page layout and desktop publishing. Harriet Dishman provided critical information about publication details.

My neighbor and friend Bill Murphy designed the book cover. Erica Johnson took the photo of my dogs and me on a walk in our favorite park.

Luree Jaquith, Betsy Sechrest, Lesley Peebles, and Peggy Potter pored over the text for countless hours as proofreaders and lent their considerable knowledge of literary and grammatical style to the finished product. I am very grateful for their patient and meticulous efforts.

# TABLE OF CONTENTS

## *Part One: Prayers for Work*

### *Everyday Prayers*

### *In Stressful Times*

# Part Two: Prayers for Healing Body and Spirit

## Everyday Healing

## In Hard Times

## Part Three: Musings and Prayers for Living

# Part Four: Seasons and Celebrations

## Winter Prayers

## Spring/Summer Prayers

## Life Celebrations

## September 11th

# Part One

---

## *Prayers for Work*

# EVERYDAY PRAYERS

---

## *About Praying for Work*

I don't really know what I'm doing right now, God.
I'm not sure I should pray about work,
or whether it makes any difference to pray at all.
I've always figured that my work was my business—
that is, my responsibility, my worldly thing.
I think it has some value for society.
I try hard to do it ethically—
even in a way that reflects what Jesus taught.

If you do intervene in people's lives,
I can't imagine that you would do it here,
where the biggest crises are important only for a moment,
and don't begin to have the weight
of the hunger and violence and tragedy
that you ... if you are there ...
must brood over daily, through the centuries.
So I'm not sure it's okay to pray here at work
or what it's okay to pray for.
Please be patient with me as I try to figure this out.

If you are all-knowing,
you must already see the true desires of my heart—
a jumble of base and selfless hopes
in which today's frustrations and dilemmas at work
are mixed with
concerns for my family and others I hold dear.
In your mercy, accept these stirrings of my heart
as my offering of the person I am right now.
In your mysterious way
amend my thoughts and desires when they are not worthy of you,
mold my intentions into actions that glorify you,
teach me how to pray to you,
and awaken my spirit to see you
and to seek your gracious, guiding presence
in my work today and always.
Amen

*         *         *

## *Before a Meeting*

The meeting I'm preparing for, God, is huge.
At least it feels huge to me as I sit here
poring over facts and ideas and proposals.
In truth, it does matter, in this microcosmic world
where I work and have so much of my being.
I've put my energy, imagination, and intellect—
and my professional pride—into this effort.
People's jobs and careers—my job and career—
will be affected directly or indirectly by what happens
in that conference room.
Do you care about all this, God?
Can this little tempest in my life possibly catch your notice,
or matter in your unfolding plan for the universe?
I don't ask for magic, God.
I don't ask you to change others' minds
or put the right words in my mouth,
without my taking responsibility for doing my best.
I do ask you to help me be aware
of your presence and your guiding hand in the hours ahead.
Give me, I pray, the humility and perspective
to seek what is good and right for all involved;
to work with my colleagues to shape a decision
that furthers the best interests of all.

If the meeting doesn't go well, God,
guard me from defensiveness or bitterness.
Master my anxiety with your peace,
release me from the imprisonment of anger,
give me the balm of forgiveness to pour over myself and others,
and teach me to trust that your mercy and goodness
penetrate every human event—
even the most secular of meetings—
with your grace, which is able to make all things new.
Amen

\*       \*       \*

## *Boss's Prayer*

Beyond all the worries about deadlines and profitability, Lord,
the thing that keeps me up at night is people.
People who need to be treated fairly,
even if decisions are disappointing to them.
People who are not performing
and worry me that I might have to let them go.
People who are in conflict,
and I must try to mediate their differences.
People whose interests differ
or whose turfs overlap.
People who are too narrowly focused
on their own responsibilities and performance
and need to work as a team.
People who are experiencing trouble in their lives
and need my prayers.
People who rub me the wrong way
yet are talented and deserve my best effort
to understand and appreciate them.
People who frustrate me
but may have things to teach me.
People I haven't gotten to know,
so don't really understand.

Help me see my job and the people with whom I work
with your vision,
which beams its acceptance and compassion
on each of your children.
Give me the wisdom and discernment
to do what is right and fair
for each person whose life I touch
in my work.
Amen

*        *        *

## *For Guidance*

With all my skills and experience, God,
I'm not sure how to handle this one.
It's a decision that will affect real people:
people I work with, people who depend on me.
Try as I might,
I cannot foresee all the consequences of this decision.
It's not a clear-cut case of right and wrong,
or good and evil;
there is a real cost—real human cost—
to each alternative.
Somehow, before deadline or crisis forces me
into a back-against-the-wall decision,
I need to sort out which good is the highest,
which alternative is most just, and most faithful
to you and to my responsibility as steward
of this business and its employees.
No matter which choice I make
and how I try to protect the people it affects,
some will be hurt, some disappointed.
I need help not only to make the decision,
but to bear  my feeling of responsibility for the costs to others.

I pray, O God,
for the perspective of faith;
for a grasp of your will in this situation,
for an appreciation of what matters most
in your scheme of things.
Make me still enough,
attentive enough
to hear your voice
and follow you,
as Jesus did.
Amen

*     *     *

## For Openness

Open me, O God,
to your Spirit flowing in and among
the people with whom I work.
Help me share my authentic self with them—
not feeling compelled to reveal the private matters of my life,
but speaking with conviction,
and listening with genuine attention.
Fill me with your passion for relationship,
that looks beyond differences and disappointments,
to see human beings struggling with their unique burdens.
Imbue my efforts to make change and take responsibility
with humility and respect.
Let me advocate for my position,
even while acknowledging the limits of my own vision,
and honoring the sometimes indecipherable
feelings and beliefs of others.

Teach me to see and delight in sparkles of grace
that bring light to an often gray workplace:
a collegial conversation,
a shared perception that brings an understanding smile,
a lessening of our guards
that slips a hint of shared purpose
and even mutual caring into a tense meeting.
Help me see afresh your image and your possibilities
in each too-familiar face.
Fill me with your Spirit, O God,
so I may face the varied moments of this day,
knowing that nothing can conquer the power of your love
where I work,
and wherever people call upon your name.
Amen

*          *          *

## Monday Morning

It was hard to get started today, God.
It's hard to switch back to being that "other person"
the professional "I" who gets things done,
who faces the world
with a competent, rational veneer.
There is the rest of me—
that is still filled with the unfinished business
of the weekend:
relationships that both enthrall and ensnare me;
casual pleasures that relax me;
time lavished or wasted on things
that matter a lot or very little;
projects that did or didn't get done;
recreation that filled my time,
but didn't necessarily fill my soul or heal my hurts;
worship that may have inspired me, or maybe not;
the stuff of my life,
aired out for two days,
and then stuffed back into the box marked "personal."

Remind me not to put my faith back in that box, God.
Help me keep it right here,
right on top of my desk, beside the phone,
next to the computer.
Teach me to trust that it is your love and righteousness
that pulls together all the pieces of my life,
that will take me through the days of this work week,
and fill them with joy and purpose and hope.
Amen

*       *       *

## *Morning Prayer for Work*

O God, whose presence makes every space sacred,
bless me in my work today.
I praise you, for your wisdom surpasses my wisest decision,
and your grace silently inhabits
the routine and mundane moments of my day.
I give you thanks for the gifts of education and experience
that make it possible for me to do my job.
I give you thanks for the many people
known and unknown to me
whose work makes it possible for me
to accomplish the tasks before me.
I confess that the details and pressures of the day
may blind me to the wonderful mosaic of Creation,
in which you use all things—even the work I do today—
to accomplish your just and loving purposes.
Make me mindful of your design for my life and work
even as I focus on the list of tasks before me.
Fill me at all times with the peace and power of your Holy Spirit,
especially when I am angry or afraid.
Make my effort and sacrifice at work today
an offering worthy in your sight.
In the name of the workman of Nazareth,
Jesus Christ, our Lord, I pray.
Amen

*          *          *

## Starting a Big Project

God, I entrust this project to you.
The size of it daunts me,
the deadline for it frightens me,
the complexity of it overwhelms me.
I know you will guide me each step of the way,
if I just turn to you and ask for help.
I know when I'm stuck,
you will roll away the stones that block me.
I know when I'm confused,
you will give me clarity.
I know when I am weary,
you will refresh me,
and give me the perseverance I need to continue toward my goal.
So I am turning to you now, as I start on this unfamiliar path.
Thank you for being a light to my mind and heart,
so I may complete this journey
and find in its end that I have been guided by faith,
and have created, with the help of your Holy Spirit,
a work that honors you
and serves my neighbor.
Amen

\*   \*   \*

## *To Be Part of God's Story*

O God,
loving creator of human history and destiny,
scripture tells us
that the people of Israel knew you to be
revealed in the events of their lives
and in the history of their people.
When we read the drama
of the parting of the Red Sea
and the resurrection of Jesus,
it's easy to forget
that the history of your salvation
is revealed also in the details of everyday life.
In the Bible,
private and seemingly insignificant acts—
the constancy of Ruth,
the curiosity of Nicodemus,
the courage of Jeremiah,
the acquiescence of Mary,
the challenge of the Syrophoenician woman—
become templates of faithfulness
and revelations of your purpose and promise.
Help us to believe,
and, believing, to perceive
that you weave the work of your kingdom
into the most mundane fabric of our lives.

Even at work,
where our days seem governed by rules and priorities
far removed from your commandments,
help us see your surprising grace,
your mysterious presence,
and your overarching purpose
waiting to be revealed in daily actions
that seem scarcely worth your attention.
Help me, and those with whom I work,
to honor you with each decision we make,
trusting that if we follow your commandments
to love you and our neighbor like ourselves,
our work will be rich with your meaning,
and our days filled with the grace and presence
of your hovering Spirit.
Amen

\*       \*       \*

## *Who Are You, God?*

Who are you, God?
I feel silly imagining you as a person up there somewhere,
yet I feel a need to address you as "You."
I can imagine you as a force—divine electricity—
ordering and energizing the universe,
but that makes me feel like an electron in a great,
impersonal science experiment.
I can feel your influence inside my brain,
when I make a decision to do what is right
or equivocate uncomfortably
when I consider doing something less than true.
But you are not in me or of me.
If anything, I am of you.
I see your power in the ocean,
your creativity in intricately designed flowers,
pollinated by miraculous living flying machines.
Are you here too? Right here in my office?
If you're present everywhere, you must be here.
Could it be my faith is not keen enough
to hear or see or feel you?
If you are here, God— and I need to believe you are—
train my heart and my soul to sense your presence
and follow your call.
Amen

\*          \*          \*

## Instant Messages

*To pray these prayers, first relax your shoulders, and draw a slow, full breath into your abdomen. As you breathe slowly and deeply, read the message.*

\*        \*        \*

Calm me down, O Lord.
Let me breathe deeply the balm of your Holy Spirit,
and entrust myself completely to your guidance and care.
Amen

\*        \*        \*

Hold my hand, O Lord, as I walk into the place of my fear.
Touch me with your presence, so I can remember I am not alone.
Amen

\*        \*        \*

I ask you to lead me, O God.
I am confused, and need greater wisdom and vision than I have.
As I stumble ahead,
I will trust you to mark my path and light my way.
Amen

\*        \*        \*

Bear my anger with me, O Lord,
so it does not turn to bitterness within,
or resentment toward those around me.
Teach me, instead, to turn its heat and energy
into a forge for justice and righteousness,
tempered by your healing gift of humility and forgiveness,
in the manner of Christ, our Lord.
Amen

\*     \*     \*

I am staggering under the load, O Lord.
I need shoulders broader than mine to get me through.
Help me summon the faith
to trust that you bear this burden with me.
Amen

\*     \*     \*

I turn this problem over to you, O Lord, for it is larger than I am.
And I submit myself to your loving will for me and for those
whose jobs and livelihoods depend on my actions.
Amen

\*     \*     \*

Thank you, Lord!
The day I hoped for has come.
Thank you for your presence with me
on the way to this moment,
and for your presence tomorrow, whatever the future may bring.
Amen

\*       \*       \*

Revive me, O Lord,
from this weariness of body and spirit that oppresses me.
Let your divine energy surround and fill me
with the hope only you can provide.
Amen

\*       \*       \*

I am so sorry, Lord.
If only the words I spoke in anger could be erased.
Give me the humility to seek forgiveness,
the patience to wait for reconciliation,
and the faith to trust in your healing love.
Amen

\*       \*       \*

Thank you for the energy in this place today, O God!
For the joy of sharing in the creation of something worthwhile,
and the delight of working with colleagues I like and admire.
Thank you for the days when work is pleasure!
Amen

*          *          *

Ahhh, Lord.
I feel so humiliated.
To have made such a mistake in front of others
is almost more than I can bear.
It is painful even to stand before you.
Comfort me in my unworthiness,
and remind me that Jesus endured the shame of the cross
to restore me to your protective and affirming love.
Amen

*          *          *

Here goes, Lord.
Be with me in there.
Help me listen with an open heart,
respond without defensiveness,
assert my point of view with respect and authenticity,
and hear your Word
even when it comes from places I least expect.
Amen

*          *          *

I'm so excited, Lord.
I've got a great idea that will really make a difference.
Help me be an effective advocate for my plan,
a willing listener, open to the suggestions of others,
and a team player honestly focused on the best outcome for all.
Amen

\*        \*        \*

I was mistreated, Lord.
The situation was unfair and the remarks untrue.
Spare me a useless obsession with resentment or retaliation.
Heal my wounded pride,
and remind me again that your perfect justice and wisdom
will ultimately prevail.
Amen

\*        \*        \*

In the midst of my busyness, O God,
remind me that I am yours;
that my work will be meaningful
when I do it in accordance with your will
and in service to you and to my neighbor.
Amen

\*        \*        \*

# IN STRESSFUL TIMES

---

## *After Being Laid Off*

Even with all the warning signs, O God,
I was not prepared.
I was not calm.
My heart raced, my head felt light and hot,
my stomach knotted,
voices sounded far away,
I was alone.
It was like the humiliation and shame of being cut from the team
in high school, only much worse.
I felt as though everyone knew,
and averted their eyes.
I know it wasn't "personal"—
they call it "reduction in force"
or "downsizing"
or "rightsizing."
But I was one of those they cut.
That makes it personal.
That makes it terrifying.
What had I done, or failed to do,
that made them decide to fire *me*?

Please be with me in this loathsome, lonely place,
O God.
Is it too arrogant to ask if this is how Elijah felt,
when he fled to the wilderness,
or Paul, when he was in prison?
In your mercy,
quiet my racing, despairing thoughts.
Give me the discipline to wait and wade through this time of
unknowing.
Comfort me when I am afraid,
keep those I love from harm.
Soothe and redirect me when I become stuck in fruitless anger.
Help me discern
amidst the wreckage of the life I knew,
a new pattern:
new risks,
new choices,
new possibilities,
a new awareness of my dependence on you,
a new hope, founded on your trustworthy and healing love,
in my work and in all things.
Amen

\*       \*       \*

## *Angry!*

I'm really pissed, God.
I'd like to yell obscenities
or pound a punching bag.
Or throw this mess on my desk across the room
and stomp on it on my way out the door.
My heart is racing,
my jaws are clenched,
and the adrenaline pumping through my system
has set my muscles and nerves on fire.
There is no excuse for what just happened.
No one has the right to treat me like that!
I feel like resigning, walking out.
Let them solve their own problems without me.
Damn them!

Whoa.
Let me try to think here.
Slow me down, God.
Help me breathe more slowly, deeply,
down to the center of my body.
Fill each breath with the balm of your Holy Spirit.
Calm my exploding synapses
with your soothing peace.

Now that the wreckage has begun to cool down,
help me determine how the fire started.
What's that, beneath the anger? ... it looks like hurt and fear.
There is my smoldering pride, which ignited
when I felt humiliated and blamed.
Here are a bunch of issues we argued about.
I can't tell from these remains which ones were worth it,
and which weren't.
It's quite a mess.
Maybe a total loss, maybe not.
I don't know what to do, God.
Whether to try to rebuild, salvage what's here,
put things back together,
or just clear it all away and make a new start.
Perhaps, some of both.
Help me be decisive now about only these things:
to ask for your forgiveness and the willingness to forgive others,
to be strengthened to do what is good and just,
and to seek your empowering love in the steps I take.
Amen

*       *       *

## *Announcing Layoffs*

Merciful God,
It is hard enough to wrestle with the uncertainty about my own
job.
It is much harder, in a way, to feel responsible
for the lives and feelings and futures
of those I've got to lay off.
Though it all comes down to "the numbers,"
they are not just numbers to me, God.
I know one has a kid in college,
another mortgage payments to make on a new house,
and each of them will be wracked with anxious questions:
"What should I have done differently?"
"Will the job market be strong enough to find a new job?"
"How long can I hold out?"
"Am I still employable?"
O God, give everyone involved
the grace to treat one another with respect,
and the honor to be both just and generous.
Help me to bear my sadness,
find words of compassion,
carry out my responsibilities
with personal integrity and faithfulness to you.
Restore my hope in your care and protection
from which nothing, not layoffs, nor mergers, nor recession
nor death itself can separate us.
Amen

*          *          *

## Disappointing news

I've just gotten awful news, God.
Oh, it's not life-threatening,
but I am so disappointed.
The future I thought I was expecting
has vanished in a airless fog of disappointment and anxious dread.
It feels like there is a vise around my head,
my stomach is churning,
and suddenly, I feel exhausted.
I'm determined not to cry, but it wouldn't take much.
How am I going to talk about this?
How can I convince myself or anyone else that
"things will be all right?"
I don't believe I deserve this, God.
It feels like I'm being punished
for something I didn't do.
In fact, I've done the best I could,
but that doesn't seem to matter to those who made the decision.
O God,
I know Jesus asked you to take his cup from his lips ...
and then obediently followed your will.
I, too, wish I could change things,
but I don't know how I will find the courage
to accept them as Jesus did,
or the wisdom to see your will in this.

Accept my pain and my bitter disappointment, God.
Accept my tears of self pity and self reproach.
Stay with me in this night of anger and anguish.
Help me sense your presence, even in my despair,
and give me faith that your Spirit will one day
guide me back to life and hope.
In the name of Jesus, who triumphed over all sin and suffering,
I pray.
Amen

*      *      *

## *During a Merger*

They call it a merger, Lord,
and say the analysts will be pleased.
I say it's chaos,
and hang the analysts!
Day after day there are "communications"
that are supposed to clarify,
but they just make us wonder
what the folks who are running this place
are thinking.
Do they have any idea what it's like
to try to run a business
under these conditions?
We make plans,
knowing that they may be meaningless
in a few weeks or months.
And there's a good chance
we won't be here to implement them, anyway.
Some new manager will come in
and undo all the progress we've made
in working together and solving problems.
It's like an invasion!
Is this what the people of Israel and Judah feared,
when foreign armies threatened them?

Oh, we won't lose our lives ...
but we will lose a part of them:
the company we've been, and believed in,
the work we've done together,
the sense of belonging and purpose
we've felt, even when frustrated
and worried about our future.
Remind us, O God,
that your loving, creating will
finds new paths in the midst of
human uncertainty;
that you use times that grieve and trouble us
to bring fresh resolve and direction to our lives.
Give us the grace to receive your direction, O God,
and the faith to believe
that you will do for us
what we cannot do for ourselves,
through Jesus Christ, our Lord and advocate.
Amen

*        *        *

## *For Needed Change*

I need a change, Lord.
I feel stale and used up.
The parts of this job I used to enjoy
seem to take more and more energy.
The annoyances that once seemed minor
are constant irritations.
There are people here I go out of my way to avoid,
and too-familiar scripts that I cringe to repeat.
I wake up in the morning with a feeling of dread.
The hours of the day seem to drag,
or are so frenzied that I am too exhausted
even to be after work.

I don't know what the change should be.
To get another job like this one
would just change the scenery
and slightly rearrange the routine.
Just to quit ... but then what?
I can't afford to do that.
What kind of change, Lord, is possible?
What do you want me to do?
How do I listen for your answer?
And how long must I wait?
When can I take the first step,
and what will it be?

I know, Lord.
Prayer is the first step.
But I'm not very disciplined,
and my faith waivers.
Help me, Lord.
You changed the lives of so many in scripture
with a word or a touch,
if they repented and believed in you.
Search me now, and show me what I need to confess and let go.
Nudge me, when I forget to pray daily
for a change of heart and mind.
Make clean my heart within me,
and renew in me a right spirit.
I beg you,
my Lord and Savior,
on whom my life depends
now and forever.
Amen

\*      \*      \*

## Hoping for a Job Offer

I jump each time the phone rings, Lord.
They said they would make a decision about this job
"in about two weeks."
Well, it's been that, and I still haven't heard anything.
Is no news good news or bad news?
Should I call and ask?
No, I've done everything I could.
I researched the company,
networked to learn about its people,
honed my resume,
practiced my interviewing,
wrote the follow-up letter,
and I have prayed without ceasing.
Getting this job would solve so many problems.

Jesus, did you ever experience this kind of fear and longing?
Did you ever dream of leaving your construction job,
and being accepted by the authorities
as Israel's teacher and healer?
Did that dream ever seem a near impossibility?
Not what I want, but what you will for me, Lord.
Please just help me out with the waiting.

If I can best serve you and meet my earthly responsibilities
with this hoped-for job, so be it.
If it is not to be,
loosen my grip on this human solution,
and thrust me forward
into a world of new possibilities—quickly, please, Lord,
quickly.
Amen

*       *       *

## *In the Midst of Layoffs*

This is a hard time, O God.
Are you here with us?
The air is heavy with the stench
of corporate casualties.
All around are empty desks of those already laid off
and skeletal departments, staggering under the added burdens
of working without colleagues and without hope.
And there is fear.
Who will be next to fall?
Will it be after the next college tuition payment is due,
or before?
We struggle to do our work,
to sell the products of a company
that seems to be falling apart around us.
Yet our conversations turn inevitably
to rumors and endless speculation.
Is there a buyer?
Will that division be closed?
What about our department?
Don't those executives know anything
about our business?
O God, we are wrapped in grief and fearful anticipation.
Is this what the people of Jerusalem felt,
as the Babylonians drew ever nearer?

Is this when Jeremiah wrote,

> *My joy is gone, grief is upon me,*
> *my heart is sick.*
> *Hark, the cry of my poor people*
> *from far and wide in the land:*
> *"Is the Lord not in Zion?*
> *Is her King not in her?"*
> *The harvest is past, the summer is ended,*
> *and we are not saved."*
> *For the hurt of my poor people I am hurt,*
> *I mourn, and dismay has taken hold of me.*
> *(Jeremiah 8:18—21)*

As you stayed with the people of Israel, O God,
stay with us now.
Turn our mourning and our exile
into the beginnings of new life,
hidden now in your mysterious future,
but promised to all who put their trust in you.
Amen

\*       \*       \*

## Installing a New Computer System:

## User's Prayer

O God,
With the power of your Word,
you created the universe.
Well, the designers of our new computer system
could sure use your help.
Seriously, Lord,
though this is no life-and-death matter,
the pressure and the anguish are building.
With each day of impasse and confusion,
the undone tasks are mounting—alarmingly—
and bemusement and bewilderment
have given way to frustration and even despair.
No one seems to know how to pull us out of this deepening mire.
Folks who used to have answers have none.
Those with authority seem hidden or hunkered down.
They make decisions that affect the rest of us
without consultation,
then blame us
for not alerting them to problems
we didn't even know they were creating.

I know Paul reassured us
that your love is greater
than all the powers and principalities of this life.
Please, please pour your love and your wisdom
on this blighted system, and on its beleaguered users.
Give to those who must fix and operate it
the courage to be humble and truthful.
Give to those of us who are caught
in this confidence-draining chaos,
the assurance that you will provide
the direction and guidance we need,
and the reassurance that our work,
though seemingly futile right now,
is still enfolded in your loving purposes.
Give us peace and patience
to do what we can do,
to turn over to you what we can't do,
and to trust that you will be
a pillar of fire by night,
and a cloud by day
to lead us through this wilderness.
Amen

\*        \*        \*

## *Installing a New Computer System:*

## *IT Manager's Prayer*

O Lord,
I know what the psalmist meant,
when he wrote that his enemies
sought his life to take it.
This system is way too big and way too complex
to come on line smoothly.
Yet the users—and they are legion—
all expect
(and to be fair, need)
to be able to get their work done now.
It doesn't help them very much to know
that within a few months, the system will be working fine.
They face deadlines today and yesterday
that are being "blown out of the water"
by the imperfections of this mammoth system.
Despite all our planning,
it has hit this institution like an asteroid.
I can understand their anger and frustration,
in part, because I'm developing a fair amount of my own.
I can relate to Elijah, who just gave up and ran away
when Jezebel threatened to kill him
after *his* effort to change the system.

Please, God, send your angels to keep me going, too.
Temper the anger of those who revile me.
Pour your wisdom and understanding,
which vastly exceed the scope or confusion
of any human system,
on me and on all those who must struggle through
this dreadful time.
Shine the calming light of your love and peace
on this tempest
which seems like eons of darkest chaos to us,
but is only a moment of change and creativity
in your eternal plan.
Forgive me for the pain I may have caused others
by my imperfect efforts to make this system work.
Forgive them, for their hostility to me,
and give all of us the grace to move forward
trusting in your love and guidance.
Amen

\*     \*     \*

## Interviewing

O Lord, I have an interview today.
It's really important. I need a job.
Walk with me into that office, I pray.
Be at my side,
and put your words in my mouth.
Keep my self-confidence from turning to arrogance;
my humility from smelling like fear;
give me a genuine spirit of understanding and curiosity
so that I may not merely make an impression,
but create a connection.
If it is your will,
make my skill and experience
something of great value to this company.
If you do not see this as the path I am to take,
help me carry out this interview
with such respect and self-respect
that it becomes not a closed door,
but a window opening onto new possibilities.
In the Name of Jesus, who had compassion
on those who sought help from him, I pray.
Amen

\*      \*      \*

## *Leaving a Job I*

I have loved this job, O Lord.
Oh, not every minute.
There were pressures and irritations
and frustrations about not always being able to get done
what I thought needed to happen.
Still, it has become a part of me:
a familiar community of friends and colleagues
with shared history and humor;
a personal vocation
that gave purpose to my work and my days;
an identity that gave me a place in the world
and a connection to something bigger than myself.
So I feel a sense of loss,
tinged with anxiety about what lies ahead.
As I leave this place,
remind me that the story I have authored here
is just a chapter in your story.
As you called Elisha out of the field
and the disciples from their boats and nets,
I trust that you call me now to find new work
and new meaning in an unfamiliar place.
O Lord, who watches over all endings and beginnings,
give me grace to grieve what I leave behind,
and give me hope to anticipate what lies ahead,
through the mercy and presence of your Holy Spirit,
Amen

*       *       *

## *Leaving a Job II*

I am delivered, O God!
I am out of here!
This job, which has cost me
so much anxiety,
so many sleepless hours,
so much frustration,
so much anger,
is over.
Praise be to God!
There are, around the edges,
a few loose strands of regret.
There are good folks I leave behind,
who will continue to work with integrity
in an organization that is not worthy of their noble effort.
There is the persisting belief in what we might have been,
and could have accomplished,
with the right leadership.
There are changes that have taken place in me.
I am less naïve, less idealistic, less open;
more aware of the need to put the concerns
of building my career and protecting my interests
on a level with doing the work of the organization.

I don't like those changes, God.
I pray that you renew in me
a sense of purpose in my work.
Help me to trust, not in the aims and steadfastness
of human structures,
but in your overarching purpose and goodness,
which lifts out of even the most broken human situations
material to build your heavenly kingdom.
You have set your children free before, O God.
As I savor the relief of freedom,
help me endure the uncertainty of
the in-between times,
the heat of the desert that I yet may cross,
before I reach the land to which you call me.
For now, O God,
thank you!
You have seen me through this far,
and I know you will continue to guide my path.
Amen

\*　　　\*　　　\*

## Starting a New Job

O God,
I know Abraham heeded your call
and went unknowing into a new land,
trusting that you would guide and protect him.
I'm not sure this new job is such a calling,
but I need you beside me and before me just the same.
I know I have skills and experience that can bring value
to this workplace.
Yet starting again
takes me back to long-forgotten anxieties of being the "new kid"
at school or in the neighborhood.
Steady me, O God.
Temper my anxious need to "prove myself"
with the patience to listen and to learn.
Help me be slow to judge,
open to new and different ways to do familiar tasks,
and sensitive to the needs and vulnerabilities of my new colleagues.
Remind me that no human situation is beyond the reach
of your care,
or outside your loving purpose for Creation.
Keep my moral compass steady,
pointed ever at the one true Word,
Jesus Christ, your Son.

And God,
as you sent angels to reassure Abraham,
I ask you to give me the vision
to see your messengers in this new place.
Whether from secretaries or vice presidents,
open me to words of wisdom and direction
that can help me grow in this job,
and make of it a vocation
through which I can serve you and my neighbor.
Amen

\*         \*         \*

## Whistle Blowing

Yikes, God.
I didn't set out to be a hero
or a villain
or a champion of justice.
In fact, I lived with the half-truths,
the willful blindness and deafness of management
as long as I could.
I tried to send up little warning flares—
more like sparklers, I guess,
because I wanted the organization,
the people I worked with and for,
to wake up and to GET IT
so I wouldn't have to,
well,
as we used to say as teenagers,
squeal.
I did, at last, what I felt compelled to do,
because I knew something had to change—dramatically.
I feel as though I've broken some sacred rule—
some Code of Silence—
that turns out to have been more important
than any code of conduct.

My anguish goes back further than that, God.
Echoes of "who do you think you are!"
and "don't be a tattletale!"
reverberate in my head.
One thing I'm not confused about, God.
It's what I learned in Sunday school.
You taught me right from wrong.
I know the difference between good and evil.
I know the prophets who warned Israel
were motivated not by their own ambitions,
but by your persistent, urgent call for justice and truth.
I'm no prophet.
But even with the dizzying amount
of criticism I've reaped
and change I've precipitated,
and with the terrible knowledge of the careers I've affected,
I wouldn't go back
to the way things were before.
I ask you, though,
as I make my way in this unfamiliar and frightening terrain,
to keep me humble and aware of my faults and limits,
to keep me safe and confident in your love,
and to guide me to discern faithfully
your will for me and for this organization
in the future that has already begun.
Amen

\*      \*      \*

## Working for a Difficult Boss

O Lord,
Help me work with the person who is driving me nuts: my boss.
In your all-knowing wisdom,
you can see how the tensions and unfairness of this relationship
are consuming my energy
and poisoning my heart with toxic resentment.
I can't figure out how to fix this, Lord,
and I can't keep living with things the way they are.
Remind me, dear Lord,
that you have more possibilities in your sight
for every situation—no matter how mundane—
than I can imagine,
and that you will give me the guidance and the courage I need
to face and to make whatever changes must come.
Help me let go of my anger
and my frantic efforts to solve the problem or assign blame.
Instead,
let me rest secure in the certainty
that you will see me through this.

Remind me that my boss shares with me
the blessing of kinship with  you.
Help me to treat my boss with love
even though we differ in opinion, temperament, and values.
Help me to "lighten up" and let go, O Lord,
so I can, with or without my boss, get on with
today's work and the work of my life—
loving you and serving my neighbor—
with faithfulness and dignity.
Amen

*　　　*　　　*

## Working With a Difficult Colleague

God of truth,
I know that she doesn't wake up in the morning
thinking of ways to thwart and unsettle me.
It sure feels like it.
How can this relationship have the power
to make me feel so lousy?
I don't want to be this angry, anxious person.
I don't want to spend my time scheming about ways
to avoid or outwit or get even.
Pour your Holy Spirit into me
as I breathe deeply and try to relax.
Help me dig deep within—
to the place where your love dwells,
and your compassion speaks.
Lead me to a place of humility and forgiveness,
so I can practice the empathy and openness
that Jesus taught and commanded.
If I cannot mend this relationship by my efforts,
give me the courage to let go,
and to trust
that you will abide with me and give me peace
even in this tempest,
through Jesus, who silenced the gale and
commanded the storm to cease.
Amen

*         *         *

# Part Two

---

*Prayers for Healing
Body and Spirit*

# EVERYDAY HEALING

---

## About Praying

Pray?

I don't know what good prayer does, God.

Maybe it's brave to have faith that it matters.

Perhaps, in a way I can't know in this life,

prayers for peace,

prayers for your loving will to be known and heeded,

create an invisible but irresistible force for good in this world.

Perhaps humble prayers for peace rise up like tendrils of hope

that get carried in the upper atmosphere of our tiny globe.

Perhaps they even neutralize

the deadly smoke of bombs and war.

Perhaps my prayers,

and the prayers of an Afghani mother whose son

is not safe in his room as mine is,

will combine in the ether of faith

to give both our sons a more humane future.

I pray that it is so.

Make me the instrument of your peace this day, O God,

whether it's in talking to a client or a teenager,

a spouse or ex-spouse,

doing a deal or looking for business,

negotiating with bureaucracies

or sitting in traffic.

Make my actions acts of prayer,
and make my prayers acts of selfless petition and hope
on behalf of all who struggle today
as members of your human family.
Amen

\*       \*       \*

## Accepting Forgiveness

God of infinite mercy,
we confess that the gift of your forgiveness
is often far down on our list of wants.
We want to be healed from pain,
cured of disease,
released from anxiety,
rewarded for hard work,
and spared the heartache of loss.
Forgiveness feels both intangible and impractical,
and requires us to admit there is something about us
that you would have us change.
Teach us not to dismiss our need for reconciliation with you,
nor to shrink from your judgment and justice,
but to find in your forgiveness
the beginning of hope and peace and joy,
through Christ who came to forgive and heal.
Amen

\*        \*        \*

*Numerous prayers in this book were written with brief introductory essays.*
*Some of the prayers that follow have such introductions.*

## Adoration, Confession, Thanksgiving, Supplication

There is a little acronym that spells out the proper order (according to someone) of liturgical prayer: ACTS, for adoration, confession, thanksgiving, supplication. It occurred to me that I had unconsciously managed to adhere to this formula in the prayers for worship one recent Sunday.

ACTS is an appropriate acronym for our private prayers as well. In our anxiety we can forget the power of faith and the gifts of mercy with which God blesses us daily. I offer these words of ACTS as a workday reminder that God is present in power and love wherever prayers of ACTS are read or spoken.

## *Prayer of Confession*

God of power and mercy,
we confess our belief that in you all things are possible,
that justice and righteousness will prevail.
Forgive us when we settle for being merely good, or good
enough.
Forgive us when we fail to seize opportunities for quiet heroism,
when we fail to challenge the routine injustices
so easy to ignore
in our work and in our communities.
Forgive us when we fail to answer your call
to engage in the great moral challenges of our day,
averting our eyes from the hungry and homeless,
allowing a comforting veil of helplessness
to blind us to our power to change the world
through faith in you.
Pour your Holy Spirit upon us, O God.
Make us improbable heroes in the daily struggle
to bring peace and compassion
to a world that longs desperately for your love.
Amen

\*          \*          \*

## *Prayer of Thanksgiving and Supplication*

O God, whose Spirit brooded upon the earth
and brought forth light and life
out of storm and chaos,
we thank you for the precious gift of this rain-driven day;
for the blessings of warmth and song and prayerful silence,
for the living presence of your Spirit
in the gathered company of your people.
Protected here in the comfortable shelter of your wings,
we don't know when or where, O God,
you will call us this week to be heroes of faith
in the great or small tumults
of the world into which you send us.
We don't know when budget decisions
or medical diagnoses, personal crises
or national tragedies
will reveal our character,
challenge our values,
and test our faith and trust in you.
We can only ask you to help us prepare for those moments
through the power and inspiration
of the One who faced death for us
without flinching or complaint.

Heavenly Parent, we pray
that the love of Christ make us
bold and constant in prayer,
generous in our habits, humble in our gratitude,
passionate in our compassion
and hungry for justice and peace;
so that our hearts may be filled with the courage
to know and to do your will
in this hour and in the days to come.
Amen

*        *        *

## Asking for Help

I have never been very good at spiritual disciplines. Spiritual impulses, yes—but daily and inward spiritual practices that don't have a tangible outcome—alas, no. I could claim walking my dogs as a spiritual practice, but in truth, if it didn't also provide needed exercise for our wild younger dog, I probably wouldn't be as faithful. And writing weekly prayers is a meaningful activity ... but would I continue to write them if no one but me knew whether I did it or not?

I have begun to recognize the challenge of a spiritual discipline that isn't, as far as I know, a typical devotional practice. It is especially fitting for me and perhaps others like me who are relentlessly task-oriented, competent, and (to appearances anyway) "on top of things." It is asking for help. I find it very hard to do.

Whatever the psychological and cultural sources of my reluctance to ask for help, there is an inescapable theological dimension to it: my anxious unwillingness to trust in God's ability and willingness to care for me, and to send others to care for me as well.

## *Asking for Help*

God, there are all kinds of risks I'm willing to take
to make things happen or to do what I believe is right.
But I falter at the risk of feeling vulnerable—
indebted, imperfect, or incompetent—
by asking for help, even your help.
Perhaps it's pride, maybe even arrogance.
I think it has more to do with fear:
fear of your not being there, or there in time;
fear of imposing,
fear of detecting a damning hint of annoyance or reservation
in the eyes or the voice
of a colleague, friend, or family member.
Help me realize that the ledge I'm standing on,
feeling autonomous but alone,
is a location of my own choosing.
And staying on it is much scarier
and riskier
than reaching out for help—
yours, and the help of those you send
to coax me off the ledge.
Amen

*         *         *

## Beginning of the Week

O God, who calls us to covenant
and who does not let us go,
be with us in the week that begins this weekday morning.
Fill us with your Holy Spirit,
and lift us beyond the spiritual stumbling blocks
that hinder us from finding peace in you.
When things are going well,
we are tempted to ascribe our success
to human skills and relationships
we believe we create and can control.
When we are in pain,
we sometimes turn to you in desperation,
sometimes turn away from you in despair,
not quite sure whether you hear our cries
or whether we deserve to utter them.
Remind us, O God,
that before the worlds were created,
before the markets dropped, jobs dried up,
cancer could be detected,
human beings invented terrible weapons,
children struggled, or relationships didn't last,
you declared your lasting and unquenchable love for us,
and set about patiently
calling the universe and all its creatures
into your covenant of self-giving love.

Call us this week, above the din of our self-talk,
out of the mire of our self-will,
to touch and become, if only for a few moments,
humble vessels of your selfless grace,
children of your covenant,
safe in the peace you alone can give,
through Jesus Christ, our Lord.
Amen

*        *        *

## *Daily Bread*

O God, whose beloved son
taught us to pray in trust for our daily bread,
remind me today that your sustenance and salvation
extend from my private cares to the global concerns
of your human family.
When there are things I can't fix,
when I am chased through the day by anxieties
that won't leave me alone,
when there is way too much to do
and no one else in sight to do it,
remind me to ask again,
Give us this day our daily bread.
Help us, who live in a world that has forgotten
physical hunger and thirst,
to remember that the bread and water
you provided so often in scripture
were but concrete signs
of the infinite love and care you have for each of us.
Remind me that you provide your miraculous sustenance
not just in barren deserts
but in organizations where people thirst
for compassion and honesty,
in families that hunger for peace,
and in crises both private and public
where people yearn for healing.

This I pray, trusting in the love of Jesus Christ,
who came to share your love freely
with all who have faith in you.
Amen

\*    \*    \*

## Dragging

It is hard, God,
when my body
is busy fighting
some microscopic invader,
and can't spare strength
for the work I've got to get done
outside my skin.
So give me energy to keep going
as long as I can, God.
Help my fuzzy brain focus
on the things that I absolutely must do,
and ignore without guilt the things that can wait.
Help my immune system fight
whatever bug this is
that's making me feel so lousy.
Help me imagine your healing embrace
as a soft bed,
ginger ale with a straw,
a hot cup of tea,
and an impenetrable nap.
I know this illness is just a slight momentary affliction, God.
So it seems wimpish to complain and ask for help.
Just for now, though,
I admit I need to be a little weak—
which is probably the way you see me
moment by vulnerable moment of my life.
Amen

*        *        *

## *For A Healthier Spiritual Diet*

Dear God,

I confess that I allow constant distractions and interruptions
to deaden my spiritual appetite. I create and consume huge quan-
tities of voice mail, e-mail, deadlines, appointments, and assign-
ments; I take on tension and stress because I am afraid to let people down.

I ask for your help, God, in making small changes to restore my
soul to health. Give me grace to do these ten things during my
day at work:

1.  To breathe deeply before and after I listen to my voice mail.

2   To thank you for being with me when I check my e-mail.

3.  To smile and relax my shoulders before I make a call or
    answer the phone.

4.  To ask for your help to "just do it" when I'm dreading a task.

5.  To accept your permission to let go of something that really
    isn't my responsibility.

6.  To ask someone who works for me or with me how they are
    doing— and really stop and listen and look at them.

7.  To give myself "time out" before I respond to something that
    provokes anxiety or anger and ask you, "God, what would
    you have me do?"

8. To write, call, or say a word of thanks to someone for something.

9. To remember that the job security and retirement you provide will never be taken away from me.

10. To trust that you love me, knowing my imperfections even better than I do; that you ask no more of me today than my honest effort and faith can accomplish; and that you desire for me to enjoy respect from those around me, moments of gladness, time for refreshment, and peaceful and restoring rest.

Amen

\*     \*     \*

## *For Endurance*

One of my favorite passages in Mark is the feeding of the five thousand. Not because of the miracle, which is magnificent, but because of the grousing of the disciples.

The disciples were suffering from serious commitment fatigue. They had just come back from their first independent preaching missions. They were very excited and told Jesus all about their deeds of power. Then Jesus said, "come away to a deserted place all by yourselves and rest a while." Ah, heaven! Much-deserved rest! Well, not only did the phone ring—but 5000 needy folks showed up on the disciples' day off.

The disciples were ticked. They wanted Jesus to send the crowd away. He pushed them to be hospitable, and they resisted, saying, "Are we to go and buy two hundred denarii worth of bread, and give it to them to eat?" (A sarcastic comment—a denarius was a day's wage; so this was more than six months of income.) Jesus kept the disciples overtime, fed the crowd, and had enough left over for his exhausted staff. Jesus, and the disciples, certainly knew what physical and emotional weariness were all about.

## For Endurance

I feel like I've hit the wall, God.
The thought of churning out one more crisp memo,
finessing one more relationship,
orchestrating one more initiative,
even returning one more phone call,
makes my blood feel like sludge in my veins.
I don't even have the energy to dream of being
on a deserted island,
because the thought of making plane reservations
and boarding the dogs just makes me feel more weary.
How did Jesus do it? How did he keep going?
How did he look into all those expectant eyes,
and not want to run away, back to the quarry,
back to being a stone mason who finished at sundown?
How did the Holy Spirit fill him up when he was past empty?
What about me? Do I dare to compare my trivial pressures
with the burdens of the Son of Man?
Ah, but Mark knew the answer:
after the crowds were fed, Jesus sent the disciples
ahead in the boat,
"and went up on the mountain to pray."
Let me go with you, Lord. Just for this minute,
let me set aside every burden,
and feel myself in prayer beside you.
Let me remember that in this place I am not alone
and do not carry my burdens alone.

Remind me that even though I may be reluctant
to pick it up again,
you will help me lift and carry my load
down the mountain,
and you will go with me
into that needy, indifferent world
where we are both called to ministry.
Lord, thank you for holding me, sustaining me,
and strengthening me to follow you
in my work in the world.
Amen

\*        \*        \*

## For Guilty Sufferers

I sustained a minor, quirky, middle-age orthopedic injury yesterday, and I am grouchy as a bear. It's not the rotator cuff, which is a good thing. However, I still have the persistent pain of a popped biceps tendon.

This is making me feel like quite a wimp, spiritually and physically. It doesn't auger well the nobleness of spirit I have always liked to imagine I would display in times of real suffering. It also makes me wonder just what God does expect of me in times of pain or difficulty. The question, "When do I deserve to complain, God?" is relevant to many of us in privileged though stressful positions. We're not alone.

> *The whole congregation of the Israelites complained against Moses and Aaron in the wilderness. The Israelites said to them, "If only we had died by the hand of the Lord in the land of Egypt, where we sat by the fleshpots and ate our fill of bread; for you have brought us out into this wilderness to kill this whole assembly with hunger."*
> *Then the Lord said to Moses, "I am going to rain bread from heaven for you, and each day the people shall go out and gather enough for that day, in that way I will test them, whether they will follow my instruction or not." So Moses and Aaron said to all the Israelites, "In the evening you shall know that it was the Lord who brought you out of the land of Egypt, and in the morning you shall see the glory of the Lord, because he has heard your complaining against the Lord." (Exodus 16:2—7)*

So the test for the Israelites was not in the suffering—God, too, figured that was lousy. The test was in how faithfully the people responded to the alleviation of suffering. That does put a different spin on things. It is okay to complain, to ask God for relief. We don't have to suffer with stoic nobility:  but we do need to accept God's mercies with gratitude and obedience.

## For Guilty Sufferers

So it's really okay to complain to you, God?
Even though this is minor,
and I've got a lot to be thankful for,
a lot more than most folks who have to deal with my problem?
So I can say this really stinks,
and you'll listen, without getting angry?
Even more astonishing,
you'll help me?
Bring me relief from my suffering?
Another confession, Lord:
I am impatient for a solution.
I don't like this pain and uncertainty.
In case I have to hang on for a while longer in this awful place,
could you send some angels to help me?
Kind friends or strangers, a doctor who knows what's wrong,
just somebody who cares will do.
Then, when relief does come,
please give me the grace to recognize it and accept it.
I know it may mean change, or even loss:
letting go of hopes I have cherished,
or living with limitations
I never had to deal with before.

Give me grace to be obedient in deliverance,
even as I have been plaintive in my captivity.
Hear my complaint, O Lord.
Take it and transform it, with your mysterious and healing love,
into joy and relief,
which I vow to celebrate
with faithful service and thanksgiving.
Amen

*        *        *

## *For the Week*

O God,
How many people each of us can be in a week:
a triumphant negotiator,
a worried parent,
a supportive colleague,
an irritated spouse,
a proud achiever,
an achy survivor,
a compassionate citizen of your kingdom,
a self-indulgent consumer,
a critic, a friend, a doubter, a believer ...
one who loves and feels loved,
one who grieves and is filled with emptiness.
Yet despite our flickering inconstancy
your infinite love is steady, sure, and unflinching.
So it is irrational of us—crazy, really—
to believe that we are the best judges
of what we need and of how the world works.
Whatever the days ahead hold for us,
help us believe that we are held in your care.
Whether struggling through sadness and trauma,
or grinding through too much work,
soaring through moments of joy
or savoring moments of success,
make us deeply aware of your sustaining presence.

Give us confidence, not in ourselves,
but in the great gift of your love,
so that we take risks
not for the sake of rebellion or personal gain,
but for the sake of your Gospel,
which has freed us from the prison of our sins,
and opened to us the gift of life abundant and life eternal,
if we but take the risk, and admit our utter dependence on you.
Amen

*        *        *

## For Those Who Pray for Others

"The biopsy results are completely benign." I was so limp by the time the doctor said this over the phone today that it hardly registered. In my mind, I had already spent a summer having radiation treatments, instead of thirty hours in a state of moderate physical and intense psychic discomfort, waiting for biopsy results that would most likely be (according to statistics) perfectly normal.

It occurred to me during this character-building, anxiety-drenched ordeal that the comfort of knowing others were praying for me—and praying hard—did not come from believing that those prayers would somehow sway the pathology report. If the cells that had grown in my body were malignant, all the praying of the last forty eight hours would not change them from malignant to benign. Instead, the knowledge of others' prayers convinced me that no matter what, I would be supported and sustained. So it's not that the prayers "worked" because the report came back clean. They worked, because regardless of the pathology report, and no matter how rough the path ahead might be, I knew God was going to be present to me through those praying hearts and hands.

Which brings up interesting questions about the effects of intercessory prayer—prayer for others. We pray for folks to get well, to get a job offer, conquer addictions, find solutions to problems that deplete them. There is evidence from scientific studies that "prayer works" to help heart patients recover sooner. I think intercessory prayer "works" because it opens up additional connections between God and the person prayed for, exactly

when the person afflicted needs it most, and may have a hard time
making that faith connection on his or her own. Though the
immediate practical outcome may or may not be a new job, a
successful cure, or a reconciled relationship, the result of prayer
offered for others is always the flowing of God's healing grace and
the spreading of hope.

## *For Those Who Pray for Others*

I pray, O God,
that when I need it most,
you will call upon others to pray for me.
I pray, O God,
that when I am needed most,
you will call upon me to pray for others.
I pray, O God,
that you will give me the wisdom and the patience
to trust that you hear each prayer,
and that you respond with your loving, healing power
to each of us who calls your name in faith.
Thank you, O God,
for those who have prayed for me.
They surrounded me with your love
at a time I certainly felt powerless,
and might have felt completely alone.
Thank you, O God,
for teaching me the faith
to pray for others,
confident that it matters,
even if I don't know how or why.

Thank you, O God,
for this deep connection to you,
accessed through our prayers for one another,
which binds us together in pain and rejoicing
and gives us strength
to face suffering,
to survive loss,
and to live in hope
that you hold our future
in your loving hands.
Amen

\*      \*      \*

## For Those with Too Much

The big economic and theological issue at our house recently was whether or not local fast food restaurants are actually extensions of our refrigerator. To wit, if you don't find something you want for lunch in the fridge, just order some for take out (or even better, for delivery). It hit a particular chord with me after Sunday's lectionary emphasis on sin and temptation. Just what constitutes unacceptable—sinful—indulgence? It's a generational thing. I routinely throw away freezer-burned, ice-encrusted remains of bread loaves that Depression-raised older folks would consider just fine for a sandwich. So how is my "wastefulness" less sinful than my son's rejection of left-over pizza?

I honestly don't know. The key thing about sin, in my view, is not determining exactly what it is, but taking part in the process of recovering from it. I actually like the idea of sin, as I understand it from our mainline Protestant perspective. It is separation from God—which can include just about anything one does on a given day. The wonderful thing is that there is a process of "divine alchemy" that can repair our souls and restore us to God, if we choose to participate in it. God is always present and ready to do God's part ... we just have to make ourselves available for the transformation.

The process goes something like this:  we sin > we confess > God forgives and gives us faith to repent through the power of the Holy Spirit > we are restored and reconciled to God, ourselves, and one another. It's not a once-and-for-all, or even a once-a-week kind of thing. It's an endless process, reflecting God's infinite grace.

## *For Those with Too Much*

I have been blessed with so much, O God.
I have health and family and education
a comfortable home and friends,
great medical care and a good job,
safe streets and plenty to eat
and more stuff than anyone really needs.
So I feel a little awkward asking you for anything else,
especially when my wants are so trivial and passing,
compared with the needs of the rest of the world.
I feel a little guilty—sometimes, a lot guilty—
for accumulating and enjoying so much wealth.
Do I dare ask you for anything?
Can I possibly deserve more help,
after you have given me so much?
With all these resources at my disposal,
shouldn't I be responsible for managing my own life?
No?
Don't you have more important things to do,
than to listen to my whining about my job?
No?
If you help me succeed, doesn't that mean someone else must
lose?
No?
How can that be, God?

*My child, my love is infinite.*
*With my love, there is no zero sum game...*
*Each act of love, each search for my truth,*
*simply adds to the world's supply of grace and goodness.*
*I am the God who set electrons in motion—*
*surely you don't think you are too small for my notice!*
*It is I who created the vastness of the universe—*
*surely you don't think you are too great or wise*
*to need or deserve my guidance and love.*
*This I promise:*
*The more you pray,*
*the more clearly you will see my presence in the world*
*and discern my purposes for your work.*
*Compared with my love,*
*the power of the mightiest executive is trivial.*
*Do not let pride or guilt stand in your way, my child.*
*Come to me honestly and humbly,*
*and I will forgive you, guide you, and bless you.*

*Amen*

\*       \*       \*

## *Laughter*

Lord,
Did laughter ever rise up
from around a campfire where you and your disciples
rested and talked?
Did you ever share funny stories
about the folks you met on the road?
Did you ever tease Peter, who so wanted to be first,
when you ate at his house?
Did you laugh and dance at weddings and village celebrations?
You must have done, Lord.
To be fully human
is to laugh, as well as cry,
to lose ourselves in moments of hilarity,
as well as in moments of prayer.
What was your sense of humor like, Lord?
Could you be funny and gentle at the same time?
Did you ever act silly,
so a sick child would stop crying
and allow himself to be held and healed?
Were you ever tempted to say sarcastic things
about the scribes or the Romans?
Remind us, Lord,
that humor can be
a healing tool or a cruel weapon;
laughter can be
a soothing balm or a poison-tipped dart.

Give us the grace to laugh
deeply and joyfully
with one another,
and refrain from laughing
at one another.
Give us grace to laugh
when we take ourselves or our situation too seriously.
And give us the gift of laughter
even through our tears,
trusting that it is a gift from you,
a rainbow sign,
that you will not leave us in sorrow,
but will lead us to eternal joy.
Amen

\*          \*          \*

## Quiet

Quiet.
Stillness.
Eyes closed,
breathing slowed,
rhythmic,
deep.
The tornado of ideas swirling in my head
spent and stilled.
In the emptiness,
thoughts sift down
and touch lightly on my awareness,
then drift away.
I breathe deeply of your healing Spirit.
I feel the pulse of life slowing,
becoming steady and strong,
calm and confident.

Quiet.
Replacing adrenaline
with divine energy;
human argument and analysis
with discernment of divine will.

Quiet.

Letting go of control of the future ...
seeking wisdom for the present,
direction for faithful decisions today.

Quiet.

Your peace, which passes all understanding.
Gratitude for the blessing
of resting in you.

Amen

*     *     *

## Restoration

O Lord,
I long to follow you to that quiet place
above the sea,
where you escaped the relentless din
of human need and expectation
to be restored and to pray.
I long to be someplace
in between the rapid-fire world where I discharge my daily tasks:
>  answering and leaving voice mail,
>  making deadlines and attending meetings,
>  picking up the kids and dry cleaning,
>  reaching in the fridge for something for dinner,
>  supervising homework and bedtime,
>  folding the laundry,
and the numb fatigue that consumes me by the end of the day.
I long to be in your presence:
>  *at rest,*
>  *at peace,*
>  *still enough to feel my breathing,*
>  *alert enough to ask for your help,*
>  *attentive to your holy and healing Word.*
Give me grace to seek and seize a few moments with you
even in the midst of it all, especially in the midst of it all.
For scripture promises and my faith affirms
that you know my heart and will give me rest
as I come to know and follow you.
Amen

*       *       *

## *Thanksgiving and Repentance*

Limitless God,
We thank you for the gift of reason,
which teaches us the workings of creation,
and the gift of humility,
which teaches us the limits of what we can know and understand.
We thank you for the gift of doubt,
which teaches us to seek the truth,
and the gift of faith,
which teaches us to live with hope and joy.
We thank you for the gift of love,
which binds us in family and community,
and sustains us in times of loss and sorrow.
We thank you for the gift of forgiveness,
which gives us second chances
and the courage to make promises
we are not sure we can always keep.
Give us grace to come before you now
with penitent and expectant hearts,
trusting your Holy Spirit to cleanse and renew us,
and ready to receive the peace of Jesus Christ,
which passes all understanding.
Amen

\*          \*          \*

## *When We Criticize Ourselves and Others*

Loving and accepting God,
day after day, we criticize ourselves and others,
confusing the blame and guilt that weigh us down
with your righteous and compassionate judgment.
Lift from us, we pray,
the burden of regret about our actions
and resentment over the actions of others.
Teach us to repent fully and forgive freely,
trusting your divine vision
to see the true content of our hearts
and to measure the true justice of our community.
Give us grace to accept and affirm one another
as beloved children of God,
and to fulfill our real vocation to love and serve our neighbor
in all our words and our work this week,
through Christ, in whose name we pray.
Amen

\*　　\*　　\*

# IN HARD TIMES

## *Cancer*

Cancer,
God.
Cancer.

Those may be the two most potent and opposing words
in the English language, O God.
Your name is the rock I cling to
as I am swept away by the fear
the word CANCER instills.
If it's not me—
if it's a loved one,
a co-worker,
a neighbor,
or even someone I don't know,
the news still shakes me,
reminds me
of all that is out of my control:
the haunting truth that even cells of my body
can turn traitor;
become hostages co-opted
by the forces of death.
Breathe slowly through me, God.
Start my heart beating again.

Wrap my shocked brain
in the warm, protective blanket of your love.
Show me the strength
I don't believe I have
to walk through this border territory
of hospital rooms,
hair loss,
exhaustion,
and the nauseating smells of illness
and intruding mortality.
Walk with me, and with all those affected by this fearsome diagnosis.
Make us faithful
to the daily tasks of our vocations,
even as our minds wander and our hearts ache.
Make me faithful
to the vocation of prayer,
with its mysterious power
that only you understand.
And give me grace
to believe the promise of scripture
that your love
has infinite and eternal power
to mend each broken heart
and broken body,
through the One who came
to heal and save.
Amen

*          *          *

## For a Parent with Alzheimer's Disease:

## Parent's Prayer

O God who forgets not your children,
remember me as the light goes dim,
and hold me tightly as I peer into the unknown.
I am afraid, O God.
Afraid of losing what I know as "me,"
afraid of letting go of what I consider mine:
my energy, my abilities, my responsibilities, my place in the world.
I don't want those for whom I have cared all these years
to have to figure out how to care for me now.
I can't imagine what meaning my life can have
if I am no longer able to do what needs to be done.
Why do you ask this of me, O God?
What is your will for me?
Why must I suffer to see ahead to the suffering that is to come?
Was this how Jesus felt, when he knelt and prayed to you,
asking to be spared the bitter cup?
I never knew I would have to walk so closely in his footsteps,
O God.
I do not feel ready or suited for this final challenge
you have set before me.
If I must drink from this cup,
release me from my smoldering, choking anger
that blinds me to the love that surrounds me.

Fill me, I pray, with Christ's unflinching courage
and serene acceptance,
so that I, too, may find in the suffering and death
I shared with Christ in baptism,
and share again with him in these days of loss,
the hope of resurrection faith,
and the blessed assurance of your love,
which does not fade even when darkness falls.
Amen

\*      \*      \*

## For a Parent with Alzheimer's Disease:

## Daughter's Prayer

Her hands, O God, held mine when we crossed the street,
picked up my toys,
poured  my milk,
clapped at my graduations,
waved goodbye when I left home.
Her hands, and the mind and heart that guided them,
have become gnarled and slow.
She sees them as useless now.
But you have given me the sight
to see how precious they really are.
You formed them, and through her love
you formed me, too.
Comfort her, O God.
As she held me when I was restless and afraid,
hold her in your loving arms,
reassure her in a voice that reaches beyond words and memory
that you are near to her,
that she is infinitely precious to you
just as she is, as she has always been.
Give her peace,
so that as twilight settles over her
she may wait with confidence for heaven-sent dreams
and your eternal dawn.
Amen

*          *          *

## For a Troubled Heart

O God who broods over the universe
and hovers near each troubled heart,
bend low
and touch me with your eternal strength
and ancient wisdom.
Loosen my fearful grip on the things that are.
Help me hold lightly the things I treasure,
so if they are snatched away,
my hands and my heart will not be crushed, but will mend,
strengthened where the scars have healed.
Help me find a few gentle souls in whom I can confide.
Teach me to cherish them as angels sent from you to feed and
shelter me in the wilderness.
Help me trust in your presence when I am really, really scared,
and dire outcomes take on a Technicolor reality
that my prayers can scarcely match.
Help me have hope
that there will be a future that holds laughter and light and joy,
even though its shape is completely obscured
behind a dark tonight and a gray tomorrow.

When good things come,
whether it's a dog's bounding pleasure
or a clearing sky
or a moment of even painful clarity,
help me be grateful
for these reminders that you are by my side,
now and always.
Amen

\*     \*     \*

## In Sadness

Is this how you felt, O God,
when Eve took that apple?
When the possibility of what could have been
dimmed and disintegrated,
and a broken reality took its place?
It's so easy for sadness to slip into despair,
O God.
Yet you did not linger there,
nor did Jesus.
You approached us again and again,
through Abraham and Moses and Elijah,
though we must have continued to make you very sad
with our petty self-will and its disastrous consequences.
Surely all those sick and sinful people clamoring around Jesus
must have sometimes overwhelmed him.
Why didn't he give up?
Why haven't you?
How can you bear the sadness of the world,
continue to pour love and hope into it,
and, perhaps, into my obscure and insignificant life?
How can I believe that it is not insignificant to you,
who bear the weight of all eternity?

Ah, Lord, you give me the answer.
I know that even in this sadness,
there exists for me a spark of your divine joy.
It smolders, and is hidden in the ashes of my discarded hopes,
but it is there.
It's not a simple promise of happiness,
but a profound sense of your presence,
that gives me life,
the certainty that I am not alone
and will never be abandoned to despair
by you who made me for your loving purposes,
and who will wipe away the tears from my eyes,
today and forevermore.
Amen

\*       \*       \*

## *Middle of the Night I*

It's almost 3am, God.
I know that you, in your sleepless mercy,
watched over me as I tossed and turned
and now fill the room with your soundless presence
even more fully than the tick of the clock
or the hum of the refrigerator.
Just as I can hear these noises now,
that in a few hours will fade into the busy hum of the day,
help me to hear your inward voice,
which sometimes gets muffled
beneath the layers of my daily concerns
or drowned out by frightening dreams or racing thoughts.
Something has awakened me—
was it your voice,
trying to make its calm and reassuring sounds heard
above the din of my anxiety,
my anger,
my ambivalence,
my sadness?
Turn my racing thoughts from painful replays of
yesterday's dramas,
from frantic schemes to fix a problem,
from imaginary battles in a war to come.

Help me instead to rest in you:
>to loosen my jaw and relax my shoulders,
>to breathe deeply and slowly of air and Spirit that
>sustain life,
>to close my eyes and feel your presence

warming and loosening the knotted and constricted places
of physical or emotional pain.
Help me to trust that whatever the daylight brings,
your loving strength will support and guide and refresh me.
In the name of Jesus, who prayed to you through the night,
I pray.
Amen

\*       \*       \*

## Middle of the Night II

Middle of the night God,
Did Moses lie awake,
wondering how he would get his people out of the desert?
Did he wonder what would happen to him
and whether he would ever get a peaceful night's rest?
How many sleepless nights
must Mary have had—
before anyone knew she was pregnant,
when Jesus was missing on the way home from Jerusalem,
when he left the village of Nazareth
to preach new and dangerous teachings?
When he was taken prisoner,
and led away by hostile, menacing guards?
So I guess you've kept lots of company
in the middle of the night, O God,
long before there were digital clocks
or late night monologues.
Please abide with me,
as you stayed with those before me.
Slow down my racing thoughts.
Calm my fear
that solutions and possibilities
will continue to elude me.

Help me trust
that it is you who hold a protective veil
over the future,
waiting to reveal it
when I am ready.
And thus reassured, grant me
some remaining hours
of blessed, refreshing sleep.
Amen

\* \* \*

## *Migraine*

God,
Migraines
are right up there with
cockroaches and tornadoes
on my list of things
creation could have done without.
They're not just headaches.
They are total system failures,
cellular earthquakes
that start at some fault line in my brain,
crush the wiring to my eyes and temples and jaws,
rumble down my neck,
and knock my stomach across the room.
Sometimes it's just a tremor,
and I can keep going.
Sometimes the world stops.
At least I have drugs,
costly pills
the managed care plans stingily dole out
that are more precious to me than gold.
They help.
But, what about all the people who suffer or suffered
without them?
What about Saul?
Soldiers and senators who can't stop?
Moms who can't afford my pricey miracle drug?

God,
could you send some angel,
some empathetic saint,
to watch over us?
To defend us from
too bright sun,
the wrong drink or drug,
too little sleep,
or emotions so powerful
our brains try
to divert them from consciousness
by brute force.

If it must be so, God:
if we must find ways to live with these
terrible beasts,
give us grace to learn compassion
for others whose suffering
in body and spirit
is even longer, deeper,
more relentless,
more life-threatening than ours.
Amen

*          *          *

## *Not Having Fun Yet!*

Dear God,
I Am Not Having Fun Yet!
To be more precise,
I'm not sure how to get through today and tomorrow.
My brain and my heart seem to have developed spiritual
arrhythmia:
working too hard, but not sustaining me,
certainly not strong enough to provide life support
for all the folks who depend on me.
I don't even want to get to the tomorrow that is coming
after a day like today.
I'd like a different tomorrow:
one in which I am well-rested
after a night of dreamless sleep;
one in which I get no e-mails that tempt me
to pound out a response that burns the keys.
A tomorrow in which everyone I depend on
offers to do more than expected
and follows through on what they have said they would do.
A tomorrow in which someone I care about,
someone who is hurting,
gets a good surprise and a new reason to hope.
A tomorrow when I have a minute to realize
*the pressure is off*, if only for a little bit,
or something just works out without having to be pushed.

In the meantime,
remind me again, God,
that you have not mistakenly put me in charge
of fixing the universe,
but have given me a divine calling card
with unlimited minutes
and free 911.
Amen

*     *     *

## *Waiting*

It's as if it were an endless rainy day, O God.
A heat wave that went on and on.
A storm at night that raged for hours, darkening the dawn.
A fever that never seemed to break.
The despair and anxiety and fear of waiting seem to go on forever.
I am humiliated, O God,
by my inability to "buck up" and take it,
to seize the power to force an answer, once and for all.
By the suspicion that I am a wimp, and others
wait in much more tortured circumstances than mine.
I fear I do not have the faith to wait with the grace I should.
As you listened with mercy to the complaints
of the children of Moses,
wandering in the desert,
or sent angels to Elijah, who had given up hope;
as Jesus appeared to his grieving disciples,
opened their eyes, and renewed their faith,
so, too, come to me in my waiting.
Do not measure my worthiness
or count against me my frantic, unknowing actions.
Give me peace to wait in quiet attention;
wisdom to discern your still, small voice
in the turmoil around me;
patience to plan with your guidance,
and courage to act with humility, honor
and decisiveness when you call me.

Remind me that your will and purpose
are both hidden and revealed in the stories of your people,
who from Abraham to Mary to Paul,
were made great not by their own might or righteousness,
but by their faithful willingness
to wait upon you, and to submit themselves
to your mercy and protection.
Amen

\*         \*         \*

## When a Friend Is Dying

Our friend and colleague is dying, God.
This is not what we know how to do.
We make deals, sign contracts,
ship orders, and calm clients.
Sometimes, in rare vulnerable moments,
we trade tidbits about our lives.

At first, there were the hospital visits,
flowers, and hearty assurances,
"you'll beat this thing."
Then there was convalescence at home,
with a laptop and speaker phone,
and we all kept up a good pretense
that things would return to normal.

Then those of us who still visited
were shocked to see how pale and thin he was.
The questions to our boss became more ominous,
"Have you heard how he's doing?"

We don't cry here, God.
Though the word is that it could be any time now.
It. Death. Trespassing on our premises.
Violating our unspoken premise
that the closest we get to life and death here
is profit or loss:
Business. Economics. The market.
Not wakes and funerals and memorial gifts,
grieving children and widows
and an empty desk,
with the skeletal remains of a once-lived life,
a box with family photos and outdated memos.

When the time comes, O God,
give us courage to grieve honestly
and to mention our fallen comrade by name.
Fill our haunted dreams
with the hope of eternal life.
Calm our terrified glimpses
into our own mortality
with a profound sense of
gratitude for life,
trust in your peace,
and faith in your abiding presence.
Amen

*       *       *

## When a Relationship Is in Trouble

I am here at work, O God,
in body alone.
My mind and heart are tangled, exhausted,
in a relationship that is deeply in trouble.
I lie awake at night,
tormented by grief and rage,
shame and fear,
while my thoughts race futilely
to find a solution
or imagine a revenge for all the pain I have suffered.
Here, where I should—must—
put away those endlessly distracting thoughts,
I am left numb and without power to concentrate
or energy to act.
Give me strength and focus, O Lord,
to do what is needed this day.
Fill me with your Spirit,
so with integrity and diligence
I may do the work you have called me to do.
In these hours while I work,
I ask you to take and hold my pain and fear
in your merciful hands.
In your mysterious ways I cannot see or understand,
I ask you to pour your healing power into this relationship
and into my soul.

Where forgiveness is needed, let it be asked for and given;
where repentance is needed, let it be sought and lived;
where anger lingers, let it be accepted and let go;
where mistrust festers, let your light of truth shine on it
and heal the wounds it has caused.
Where an ending is near, let me face it with courage.
Most of all, Lord, let your intentional love,
which honors and protects all persons equally,
guide and direct my actions.
Remind me that your will for us
is to love kindness, do justice,
and walk humbly with you
in each human relationship,
whether it flourishes or fails.
Keep me from the sins of arrogance and despair.
Call me again to put my trust in you,
my certain hope and consolation,
whatever the future brings for me,
and for all those
who are affected by this sorrow and struggle.
Amen

*          *          *

## *When in Pain*

God of mercy,
who sent Jesus to touch and heal us,
comfort me with your soothing grace.
I do not know where my physical pain ends,
and the pain of my soul begins.
Together
they have kept me up at night
and stolen my concentration by day.
Stay present to me,
you alone who can heal my heart and body.
Penetrate the tissues and cells that ache
with your healing light,
which shines neither hot nor cold,
but radiates love and truth.

Jesus, Gentle Savior, hold my hand
and give me courage to look and listen for
the truths hidden at the edge of my consciousness,
truths I may have tried to silence
because I am afraid they will upset others.
Strengthen my spirit so I can lift from my body
the burden of voicing my pain.
Help me accept your love for me
as permission to love myself,
to take the best care of myself
that human wisdom and medical skill allow.

I beg you, Lord, to create a space
for laughter and silliness
where the pain is not overwhelming.
Finally, loving God, give me hope
through Christ's resurrection,
to believe the pain I know today
will be transformed through your mysterious power
into a new life of love and joy.
Come quickly, O Lord, and deliver me,
for in pain I cry unto you.
Amen

\*       \*       \*

## When Worried about Others

My heart is full of worry, Lord.
Would that I could run to you
as Jairus did,
and beg you to come heal with your touch
those I love
who suffer in mind and body.
Yet I am here, trying to do a job
that right now seems
a meaningless trifle
compared to the weight of deep fear and agony
that bends my spirit.
And you ... you no longer walk the streets
of the next village,
or preach from a boat
in a nearby cove.
How can I find you?
How can I, who have been given too much and have
given too little,
deserve to ask you for this impossible gift of grace?
Release me, my Lord,
from the burden of demanding certainty
and the fear of being unworthy,
and breathe into me the refreshing and calming breath of faith,
so that I may again know and understand
the promise of Easter:

that through the power of God,
you have broken the grip of sin
and conquered the finality of death
for all time and all people.
Be with me as I toil this day.
Tenderly comfort and give your healing peace
to those whom I hold dear
and entrust to your merciful and eternal care.
Amen

\*       \*       \*

# Part Three

---

*Musings & Prayers*
*For Living*

## *Balance*

I wonder if everyone my age (Middle Bronze Baby Boom) has an emblematic sitcom episode from childhood. Mine is an episode of *The Danny Thomas Show.*

As I recall, Danny played a New York variety show host with a Cuban doorman. In my signature episode, Danny is running a talent contest for kids, and his Cuban doorman's son is scheduled to audition. The young boy is an accomplished dancer, but very shy. He arrives at the studio before his audition to wait for his dad, who is supposed to come with the music for the band. While he waits, another boy performs a very fast-paced tap dance. Dad doesn't arrive in time, so, in a panic, the boy indicates to the band that his music is the same as the previous performer's. He starts, but doesn't have a clue how to tap dance so is hopelessly lost and embarrassed.

In the midst of this excruciating scene his dad arrives, gives the band the proper music, and the boy is transformed from a helpless duffer into an accomplished Spanish classical dancer— which is what he knows how to do.

This episode has come to mind a lot recently, as I've tried some new things at work, at which I don't feel particularly adept. At the same time, I recently observed the eighteenth anniversary of my ordination, and I am pleased to realize that I'm still doing things that are new and challenging, even though I'm in the same job, same office. Sometimes, of course, new and challenging things are thrust upon us—like hunting for, or starting, a new job. Or staying in the same job and acquiring a new corporate owner. Trying to seem competent and under control in those circumstances can feel like trying to tap dance when what you know how to do is ballet.

It seems that in both our work and our personal lives there is a balance to be struck between the confidence of working from our existing knowledge and experience base (there have to be some consolations of accumulated age) and the challenge of stretching to try new things that may feel scary and awkward. Too much of the former is stultifying (though I'd settle for a day like that now and then) and too much of the latter is exhausting.

So one of the things that I pray for all of us who are at work today—whether in an office, or in school, or at home parenting—is a blessed balance between the comfort of competence and the exhilaration of creation and change.

## Balance

Creator God,
How I love new ideas!
I've learned they have their liabilities, though.
As we saw in the race toward Baghdad,
if you're too far out in advance of your support,
you can end up strapped for food and water
and vulnerable to attack.
I've realized that it's good to go for something new
with a friendly colleague
who "has your back"
and cheers you on.

Then there are times
when learning new things is thrust upon us:
messy times when parents are aging,
kids are hurting,
marriages are failing,
jobs evaporating,
and even with all our skill and effort
we feel like we're stumbling through a complicated new dance
or trying to speak a foreign language.
So God,
When you created earth,
did you really mean for human beings
to be your collaborators in creation?
That's an overwhelming job description, God.

At the same time,
it is pretty exciting
to be doing a new thing
that just might be part of your plan
for your new creation.
This I pray:
please remind me to ask you,
when I'm doing a new thing at work or at home,
whether my goals are worthy
and my means acceptable in your sight.
And please let me know
what music you intend for me to dance to.
Amen

*        *        *

## Courageous Faith

It takes courage to have faith. That's what we tell our confirmation class as they wrestle with the first few chapters of Genesis, which lay out most of the great and unanswerable theological questions: order vs. chaos, good vs. evil, knowledge vs. innocence. These are all subsumed under the Big Question: the nature of God and of God's relationship to creation.

Our young scholars ask all the right questions: "If God created everything, did God create evil?" "If God plans everything, why do bad things happen? Does God plan those?"

I often feel like a snake oil salesman who's been challenged to back up the outrageous claims for his product when I am faced with their questions. My answers seem partial and tentative, compared to the weight and depth of the questions. I guess I'm not alone. Saint Paul writes to the Corinthians,

> *For now we see in a mirror dimly, but then we will see face to face. Now I know only in part; then I will know fully, even as I have been fully known. (1 Corinthians 13:12)*

We get tired of this "not knowing" stuff—not knowing about our jobs, the economy, war in Iraq, our parents' failing health or our own health, our teenagers' ability to make reasonably good decisions, our next moves in difficult relationships, the source of our next client. In life's daily uncertainty, it takes courage to have faith that it matters to God, and that God will act.

## Courageous Faith

O God,
Some of the problems we face
hardly seem worth your notice,
and some seem beyond your power or design to fix.
We spend endless hours worrying about the former
and run away in despair or denial from the latter.
Help us to let go of the little ones
and to act more like people of faith in facing the others.
Remind us that you don't measure human problems
by the pound or dollar, mile or teardrop,
but by the earnest desire to seek your help,
and do your will.

Right now, O God,
both our little problems and the big problems that surround us
seem overwhelming.
In fact, they intersect.
Worry about the sluggish economy
and the effects of war here and abroad
pulls on all of us like a giant vacuum,
sucking away the dreams of families,
the budgets of businesses,
the ability of hospitals, governments, and charities
to care for the sick and poor and vulnerable.

Hold us steady, O God,
who have been accustomed to being so confident
in our skills, assets, and accomplishments.
As we face the raw uncertainty of our human condition,
give us courage to trust what we can see but dimly,
but shall someday see face to face:
your goodness, grace, and glory.
Amen

\*       \*       \*

## Dragon Slaying

I confronted evil this week. Evil is clever. It disguises itself in all kinds of ways. It attaches itself to people who really aren't all that bad. So they confuse us. We're not sure they mean to do harm. Sometimes, evil co-opts people who mean well, but lose sight of what's most important. Sometimes, those we hoped we could trust to "do the right thing" just don't do it—for reasons we can't fathom. A hymn in our new hymnal has a wonderful verse that speaks to evil's chameleon-like quality:

> *Old aching God, gray with endless care,*
> *calmly piercing evil's new disguises,*
> *glad of good surprises, wiser than despair,*
> *Hail and Hosanna, old aching God!*

I have a disabled friend who was harmed by a combination of institutional negligence, callousness, and ignorance. The indifference of those who were responsible had brought him almost to tears of frustration. Digging deeper, he found a state regulation that spoke to his situation, and suddenly he felt he had the law in his hand and on his side. He had a new sword to use in his very real fight against intimidation and injustice. After a hard week, it felt as though God had given the good guys a victory. That gives me and others the encouragement to keep at it next week, and the week after that.

## Dragon Slaying

God, I know you were with me
when my nemesis tried to stare me down
tried to twist the facts
and shake my convictions.
I know you were with me
when others backed away
because the issues were too hot
and too threatening to the status quo.
I know you were with me
when I heeded advice to be cautious
and seek constructive solutions,
and you were also with me
urging me not to let an issue
that affected people's lives
slip
   off
      the table
because no one else wanted to address it.

Thank you for courage, God.
Thank you for small shoots of righteousness
poking up among weeds of indifference.

Remind me to let go for now, God.
Let me laugh a little and forget a little,
trusting that the power of justice
rests surely and eternally in you.
And you will be there to sustain me
next time
it's time to slay a dragon.
Amen

\*     \*     \*

## For Economic Life

It's easy to see the need to pray for economic recovery: for the return of confidence to corporate board rooms where investment and employment decisions are made; for an expanding economy that creates new jobs, lessens state budget deficits, restores stability to the stock markets, and rescues families from unemployment and financial crisis.

It is also pressing to pray for ethical decisions and actions on the part of corporate executives, managers, and accountants. We need to pray for restraint, humility, and a spirit of generosity and responsibility among corporate leaders, some of whom, in recent years, seem to have been on a long binge of unrestrained greed.

Which brings us to the really tough economic issue, from a Christian point of view. Greed. Needs versus wants. It's a central— perhaps it's the central— dilemma for Christians who participate in a free-market economy (or, if you prefer, a regulated capitalist economy, which is a more accurate description of what we have on our hands).

When Adam Smith "discovered" supply and demand and offered his history-changing analysis of a hypothetical pin factory (for a refresher, see that Economics 101 staple, Robert Heilbroner's The Worldly Philosophers), most people were poor, hungry, cold, uneducated, and ill-housed. Subsistence farming was the dominant form of economic activity. Economic specialization, industrialization, and a free market could, by increasing productivity and encouraging folks to act in their own self-interest, raise the standard of living for everyone.

Through the eighteenth, nineteenth, and most of the twenti-
eth centuries, this new economic engine created huge benefits by
raising living standards, educational levels, life expectancies, and
other "quality-of-life" measures for Western society.

Fast forward to the early twenty-first century. With all its
changes, the economic engine still requires a continuous cycle of
producing and selling more stuff, more cheaply, to more people.
We all wait breathlessly to hear whether Walmart has had a good
December, because measurements like that affect consumers' jobs,
spending, and home owning, as well as firms' investment decisions
and employment decisions.

The moral problem arises when the "stuff" produced and
bought is no longer the basics of decent housing, enough food,
adequate education. How flat does a flat screen TV need to be?
How many more clothes can I cram into my closet? How many
more video games can I be suckered into buying? How much
does my sometimes frivolous consumption benefit folks truly in
need in our country and in developing nations? What about prof-
its that go into those huge corporate perks—stock options, bonus-
es, and private jets—self-interest on steroids—that are supposedly
the fruit and the motivator of competitive excellence in a market
economy?

There is no easy answer. The health of our economy
requires continually rising consumption by folks who don't need
more stuff. Economic rewards in a market economy are often lopsided and sometimes unjustified. The benefits of economic growth

in the U.S. are only imperfectly felt by those who need them in
other countries. Even when it prompts free-trade agreements and
economic reform in third-world countries, it's not clear how well
the "trickle down" theory really works. Economists and Christians
alike debate the ethics and economics of corporate expansion in
developing countries. What some see as sweat shops, others see as
sources of increased freedom and economic power.

The dismal success of planned or socialist economies shows
us that, with all its flaws, a market economy delivers more
"good"—less hunger, better housing, better health care, higher life
expectancy—than the alternatives. Faced with this dilemma of
good (plenty and freedom from want) and evil (the sins of greed,
gluttony, and injustice) inextricably bound together, sometimes the
only thing to do is to recognize the moral ambiguity of our economic system and our part in it, and to pray for wisdom that transcends individual human beliefs, biases, and desires, as we wrestle
with our personal and economic choices.

## For Economic Life

Patient God,
The way the Bible puts it,
it started with Adam and Eve.
This drive of ours to want and to have.
We've found some ways to put this energy
to work, to provide for ourselves and others,
in a complicated dance called a market economy.
But is it energy, or is it sin?
Despite our higher goals
the dance can become demonic
and the outcome
completely unlike the lofty, or at least benign,
ballet we choreographed.
Wise, patient God,
You know we can't resolve this dilemma
by taking refuge in absolutes or in simple solutions.
Laws and regulations cannot replace moral character,
and market forces do not guarantee justice.
We can't compensate for outsized corporate greed
by large-scale charity.

So as we lead or manage, invest or sell, vote or influence,
buy or save,
as we decide and act
as managers,
parents,
homeowners,
citizens,
help us to remember the words of Micah:

> *With what shall I come before the Lord,*
> *and bow myself before God on high?*
> *Shall I come before him with burnt offerings,*
> *with calves a year old?*
> *Will the Lord be pleased with thousands of rams,*
> *with ten thousands of rivers of oil?*
> *Shall I give my firstborn for my transgression,*
> *the fruit of my body for the sin of my soul?"*
> *He has told you, O Mortal, what is good;*
> *and what does the Lord require of you but to do justice,*
> *and to love kindness,*
> *and to walk humbly with your God?*

*(Micah 6:6—8)*

Amen

\*          \*          \*

## *Fearfully and Wonderfully Made*

One of the privileges of being a pastor and a counselor is to behold the complexity and courage of ordinary human beings.

I was mindful of this privilege this spring, with its year-end rituals: the final essays of our confirmation class and graduations that mark the ends of an era of family life. There was also a sprinkling of small and moving funerals. I was reminded that living and continuing to love and laugh in the face of complicated and heartbreaking realities is in itself a huge act of courage.

I am also working on the twenty-fifth reunion of my class in business school. There were only forty-seven of us—the first class at the Yale School of Management—and our two years together were very intense. In retrospect, I realize I was almost completely clueless. I was focused almost exclusively on being the best and brightest, and I sure missed a lot of important details. As I send out e-mails, I am aware that these are talented, interesting, and complicated people, about whom I know only the most superficial details. So the reunion is an opportunity for me to go back and connect in a new and more—what—authentic? meaningful? mature? way with people who were very important to me.

In many management and community settings, we relate to people in a narrow, functional way. Whether it's on the executive committee of a bank, on a volunteer town board, or in an impersonal transaction at a grocery store checkout counter, we ask the question "Will she get the job done?" without asking the more important question, "Who is she, and what is affecting her life right now?" I believe we diminish our effectiveness both as managers and as Christians when we do that. We miss out on the human stories of loss and accomplishment, fear and joy, courage and faith that bind us into community and inspire us to laugh and pray.

The psalmist says in Psalm 139,

*I praise you, for I am fearfully and wonderfully made.*

It's true of each of us. An important part of our vocation as Christians is to discover and celebrate that—in ourselves and in others with whom we live and work.

## *Fearfully and Wonderfully Made*

Wise God,
How amazing
that you could call into being
billions of people throughout the ages
and fashion each one uniquely.
Each one, like some rare
precious stone found in a creek bed,
with only a small bit of granite worn away here or there
to reveal what is underneath.
All those people I write off or don't even see
in the course of a day—
those who irritate me at work
or seem rather dull,
talk too much or call at the wrong time,
work as parking attendants
or compete with me and maybe even threaten me.
Each one
is vulnerable and courageous
in ways I can't see or even imagine.
It's so tempting, from where I sit,
to envy some as fortunate
and to ache for some who seem
unfairly burdened.
You, O God, see it all,
and make sense of it in a way
that makes no sense to me.

Save me from the presumption
that I can ever know
exactly what weight someone else is bearing,
or why he does what he does.
Fill me with curiosity
about the lives of people you have chosen
to share my path for a while.
Give me grace
to draw inspiration
from those who have the courage
to keep going,
who refuse to let disappointment or confusion
settle like silt on their hearts and dim their senses,
but stay alive to sunlit flashes
of your joy, hope, and love.
Reveal to me this day
the wonder of your creation
etched in the private courage and
imprinted in the spiritual DNA
of each person you have formed
from human clay.
Amen

\*　　　　\*　　　　\*

## For Imperfect Lives

"Everything will turn out all right" strikes me as one of those pernicious falsehoods right up there with "college is the best four years of your life." The problem is with the word "everything." It suggests a degree of completeness, harmony, and resolution that is, in my view (both theological and personal) unknown in the human condition or the created order.

Some things do turn out, thanks to the grace of God in the form of small miracles and acts of human kindness, often combined with the application of human effort and skill. There are moments of delicious enjoyment, exquisite relief, deep satisfaction, and plain old contentment. These precious moments are constantly colliding with confusion, new complications and losses, and disappointments. Many of us take the messiness personally. We figure it's due to something that is wrong with us, our spouse, our kids, the schools, our parents, the company or organization we work for, a bad boss, or a bad hair cut. And we believe, with a certain amount of secret shame, that other folks somehow do it better than we do. They don't suffer from the same disorderly aggregation of aggravation and doubt.

Though I get trapped in that thinking time and again, I know from my experience as a pastor that it just isn't so. Anyone who appears to have a perfect life doesn't. Even folks who seem to cope with stuff with more strength or confidence than we do, who seem to get better breaks, or (even more maddeningly) who seem to do just fine and avoid the doubt and introspection that plague us, are only enjoying a temporary, and perhaps illusory, respite from the inevitable hardships of life.

The great thing about acknowledging this inherent imperfection in all of life is that it sets us free. Free from the expectation that there is a way to "get it right." Free from the belief that we are more flawed or damaged or less worthy than others. Free to accept our common humanity, to accept others who are more like us than we wish: folks whose visible scars of poverty or oppression resemble our hidden ones. And free to accept others who intimidate us with their seeming invincibility, because we recognize that their vulnerability simply lies hidden from our view.

Jesus saw through it all, of course. And still does. He recognized posturing and exposed it; he also saw through layers of shame, despair, and rejection, and brought forth love and hope in the most miserable sinners. Long before the twelve-step groups latched upon it, he urged his followers to take one day at a time.

*So do not worry about tomorrow, for tomorrow will bring worries of its own. Today's trouble is enough for today." (Matthew 6:34)*

## For Imperfect Lives

God,
You made me, so you know how nearsighted I am.
It doesn't surprise you that there are moments
when my situation looks to me like it will last forever,
and I can't stand it for one more second!
I look at other folks who seem to be doing just fine,
and I feel like such a loser.
I'm convinced that they get more done,
have fewer loose ends,
and never run out of energy or enthusiasm.
They could easily avoid this conflict with my boss or client
that's making me a sleepless wreck.
They probably have great marriages
or the gumption to get out of bad ones.
They probably have all their photos in photo albums, too.
Why can't I do all that?

Remind me again, God,
that our baptismal questions end with the words,
"as best you are able,"
and I answered, "I promise, with the help of God."
Remind me that those other folks are near-sighted, too.
One or two of them might even be looking at me,
believing that I know just what I'm doing.
When I start anxiously trying to anticipate the future
or to compare myself to others,

pull me back to the here and now, and to you.
Remind me that I am exactly where I need to be,
and I can do all you expect of me.
Tell me again that you are here with me
and will walk with me through this valley, then through the next,
giving me what I need, and helping me to recognize it clearly
in faith and prayer.
Amen

\*        \*        \*

## Grounded

It's Sunday night and I've been grounded. Quite literally, actually. My new minivan with 246 miles on it is resting fitfully at the body shop at Brigham Gill Autos. Physically I'm fine, and I'm quite fortunate that the large, heavy pick-up into which I skidded had a large, heavy bumper that hit above my air bag sensor. Otherwise, said my friend the officer who came to my aid, the air bag would certainly have gone off as the hood crumpled.

The "proximate cause" of my accident was the classic lavender VW bug that arrested my eyes for just a moment too long. However, even before the crunch,  my "observing ego" had been sending up warning flares:  I have been too busy, firing too long each day on too many cylinders. I have too many things on my mind. Worthwhile and unavoidable things—unscheduled trips to the vet and the dentist along with meetings, memorial services, and home responsibilities. Still, too many things.

It gives me some empathy with the numerous seventeen- and eighteen-year olds in our parish who have, in recent months, gotten themselves in the local paper's police log for acts of over-reaching stupidity. That was actually what I had been thinking about before the lavender Volkswagen. Their sense of power and independence gets them in all kinds of trouble. I've been feeling a little of that, because recently I've really felt I was "in the zone" and I've been relishing the ability to keep going and going... until this afternoon.

So now I have to stop ... and take stock. Set some limits. Subtract rather than add. Funny, how being grounded is the end of the world when you're a teenager, but being grounded, having a sense of your limits and some perspective on what's important, is a state to be sought and longed for when you hit your fifth or sixth decade. Here's to being grounded long enough to learn mindful living... and driving.

## *Grounded*

God,
There's a part of me that still wants to fly.
That still dreams—waking and sleeping—
of being able to meet every challenge,
pursue every great idea,
answer every urgent need.
That wants to inhale the energy of life whole,
without slowing down to digest it,
without resting twenty minutes
before going back in the pool.
I need your help, God,
to learn to stop
before I am scary-busy.
Before I become too preoccupied
to STOP in time
to keep myself healthy,
to listen to someone I love,
to do something that is not work,
not necessary,
not earnest,
and not, not
an effort.

I need you, God,
to take away the car,
turn off the phone,
close my e-mail,
clip my wings
and remind me that sometimes I need to feel
small and not in control.
To tell myself and my friends
that my heavenly parent says
I'm grounded.
Amen

\*          \*          \*

## Guilt and Grace

The lectionary readings this past Sunday led us into the difficult territory of guilt and grace. This dichotomous pair is probably my least resolved theological push-me-pull-you. Even now, I am torn between the oppressive prodding of what I feel I should do, and the lure of what I feel I really need or want.

So at the beginning of the work week, I hope you will stop yourself in mid-thought when you are about to chastise yourself for a detail overlooked, a call not quickly returned, a need not anticipated (someone else's) or acceptable (yours). Fix in your mind that image from the Nestea ice tea commercial: the one with a hot, sweaty, lawn-mowing suburban home owner plunging deliciously into a pool. It's a great illustration of God's grace. And whatever the week brings, may you remember that it is filled with God's grace, offered freely for you to accept and share.

## Guilt and Grace

Patient and merciful God,
We don't know what to do with guilt and sin.
We feel guilty a lot, but maybe it's about things
that don't matter much to you.
We are often perfectionists,
but careless of the cost to the people
we neglect in our quest for perfection.
We feel horrible about the suffering in the world,
but let sports and a host of other distractions
interfere with our chances to serve the poor.
We are in a muddle, O God, from which only you can lift us.
So for these moments
release us from the burden of our bad feelings and negative
thoughts.
Fill us with the quiet joy, the peace that passes all understanding,
of resting in the knowledge that we are wholly forgiven,
and freed to embrace new life.
Help us begin that new life this day, this week.
When we are sad or afraid, remind us that you are beside us.
When we are irritated or judgmental,
help us hand our frustration and judgment over to you,
so the relief and release
of your compassion and acceptance
can flood our hearts and bodies.

When we look at the world and feel despair,
give us courage to hope,
and to take small concrete steps
to alleviate suffering and create understanding.
This we pray,
trusting that we are redeemed by Christ's death and resurrection,
and filled with the power of the Holy Spirit
to be his presence in the world.
Amen

\*     \*     \*

## Leadership, or the Downside of Being a Duck

Ducks make everything look easy. They swim, dive, fly, dash across a lawn, or hop onto aquatic B&B's (floats and docks) for the night. They are especially great swimmers, moving smoothly through the water, and lifting almost instantly into hovercraft mode when something (in our case, a dog with delusions) gives chase. There is a catch. Ducks only appear to glide effortlessly along the surface. Meanwhile, they're paddling like mad underneath.

In my experience, being a leader of an organization or household or project is a lot like being a duck. You have to do all kinds of things competently, look poised and confident as you rally and lead the troops. All the while working like mad (and sometimes, worrying like mad) underneath the appearance of calm.

Ducks at least have the sense when flying south to take turns at the front of the V and give the leaders a rest. Leaders in human organizations and families don't often get that break—or believe they are allowed to take it. The higher the level of leadership, the greater the pressure for a constantly flawless and perfectly composed performance. Ducks would think we're nuts.

## *Leader's Prayer*

God,
Please remind me,
next time I'm really tired
from flying out in front,
that you always go before me
to push away obstacles,
like air,
that I can't even see.
When I feel that there is
no one I can turn to
to confess my fears and fatigue,
remind me
that even Jesus
accepted help from the disciples
and from you.
Help me learn, eventually,
that you are undaunted
even by my biggest deal,
by this crucial meeting,
or by that command performance.
Remind me
that the first commandment of life in the fast lane,
"Thou shalt be cool and in control"
is not from you.

Help me learn from Jesus,
that new life and unimagined possibilities appear
when I stop trying to paddle so hard,
fly so high,
or seem so strong,
and let you ask others
to take their turn in front.
Amen

\*     \*     \*

## *Moon Shadow*

Yesterday my short afternoon trip to the office "to get a few things done" turned into a marathon, and by the time I left it was really too dark to take my dog for a walk in the park. This was a particular problem yesterday, because I had only the older dog with me, who was having "quality time" with mom before her younger sister returned from the northern woods. Not taking her for a walk would be like welshing on a promise to go to the circus with a five-year-old. Off we went with a dying flashlight. Seemed an apt metaphor for my almost-but-not-quite prepared state in life.

The park is hilly with footpaths traversing it. Part of it is covered by large meadows, and some is deeply wooded. The largest hill has a long, winding path through the woods. I figured we could at least walk over the meadow.

Do you remember the Cat Stevens' song from the early seventies, "Moon Shadow?" Yesterday after dark, the moon was so bright that it was actually casting a shadow. Moon shadow. At the beginning of our walk, some puffy clouds over the horizon were still tinted pink from the sun, and the moon was brilliant. The beauty was breath-stopping. We crossed the meadow and reached the path that winds up the hill through the woods. With leaves safely underfoot for the winter, the moon shone through the trees and easily illuminated the path. Some of the leaves on the ground actually glowed with reflected moon light. As I neared the top of the hill and came out into the meadow, I suddenly remembered the words of Psalm 121,, written upwards of thirty centuries ago.

They are still precious and powerful, and at that moment, they were spectacularly alive with God's presence and promise. I pray that God guides and illuminates your path this week, wherever it leads you.

## Psalm 121

*I lift up my eyes to the hills—*
*from whence will my help come?*
*My help comes from the Lord,*
*who made heaven and earth.*
*He will not let your foot be moved;*
*he who keeps you will not slumber.*
*He who keeps Israel*
*will neither slumber nor sleep.*
*The Lord is your keeper;*
*the Lord is your shade at your right hand.*
*The sun shall not strike you by day,*
*nor the moon by night.*
*The Lord will keep you from all evil,*
*he will keep your life.*
*The Lord will keep your going out and your coming in*
*from this time on and forevermore.*

## Nonagenarians

I conducted the funeral of a magnificent 97-year-old named Howard today. It was another confirmation of my theory about folks who live well and fully into their tenth decade.

I figure many of us can get to our 80s with a combination of good genes, good living, and good medicine. To live—really live— into your 90s takes something else. You could call their secret the ten spiritual habits of successful nonagenarians. All of the unusually vibrant ninety-somethings I have buried in the last few years embraced and embodied these qualities. (It is possible to creak into one's 90s being crotchety and irritable, but that's the subject of a different prayer.)

1.  They achieved unusual goals early in life. One woman graduated from Smith College in chemistry in 1926. Another went from singing professionally on Broadway to becoming a doyenne of the ballet and theatre world. Howard, the grand old gentleman
    I buried today, turned down his dad's offer to pay for Harvard or MIT. Instead, he paid his own way though school and graduated valedictorian in the class of 1926 at Massachusetts School of Pharmacy, where he later taught, became dean, and finally,
    president.

2.  They keep doing amazing and meaningful things. The Broadway dancer-turned-ballet-teacher received her doctorate in theater arts at age seventy. The Smith College chemist walked up the steep path to her cottage at

Sunapee when she was ninety-five. The pharmacist continued to run and teach continuing education for pharmacists for decades after his retirement.

3. They stay involved with the world. Howard read five newspapers every morning before 9AM until well into his nineties, and continued to discuss current events with his family until the end of his life.

4. Throughout their lives, they accept change and face adversity with courage. Nonagenarians don't have more trouble-free lives than the rest of us. My small sample has lived through illness, loss, betrayal, and the deaths of loved ones, in all periods of their lives. They simply accept their share of adversity without resentment, then find ways to adapt and live beyond it.

5. They accept the infirmities of old age with grace and perseverance. No matter how strong one's spirit, things break down when one hits ninety. So they are not spared infirmity. But they welcome whatever medical interventions can help them, and they continue to live as fully as they can with the limitations their conditions impose. Then they accept dying with matter-of-fact calm and, sometimes, even with impatience.

6. They embrace surprise. Fabulous nonagenarians love parties and surprises.

7. They laugh easily and keep their sense of humor well exercised.

8. They stay lovingly and generously involved with family and friends of all ages. They are wonderful grandmothers, great-grandmothers, uncles, or aunts. They are interested in the goings-on of younger generations, neighbors, new and lifelong friends. They love to share their know-how, their wealth, and their stories.

9. They love life and rejoice in the accomplishments of others.

10. They trust the future. Though many are private about their beliefs, they trust God and God's goodness. They hope for eternal life, and do not fear death.

## Nonagenarians

Generous God,
thank you for the inspiration
of long lives lived fully and well.
Thank you for wrinkles and thin, snowy hair
and intriguing stories.
Thank you for their power to remind me
that this season's crisis
is but a moment
in a long life that
I can choose to shape (or not)
in the image of these everyday saints.
Help me look to these pilgrims before me,
as I look toward the second half of my life.
Like them, let me spend my time and effort
on work that has meaning for me,
and benefit for the world.
Keep me curious.
Help me learn to use at least one new technological marvel
each year, even if it's last year's marvel.
Make me listen to one new song on the radio
all the way through, and say that I like it.
Keep me thankful for pills and doctors.
Help me accept the bitter and broken pieces of my life
as ingredients in your rich, original recipe for me.
Lead me to rejoice without looking back,
or without anxiously scanning the horizon before me.

Remind me that each day,
each smile,
each breath,
is a gift from you, given to me to use and share with joy
and with trust in the power of your love.
Amen

\*          \*          \*

## *Oops*

I'm so glad I am twenty years older than I was the last time I felt this way. Back then I was facing an angry client whom I had assured of some completion date, only to have the art department (which reigned supreme in our small ad agency) inform me that the client couldn't have what he wanted when he wanted it. Wow. I can remember picturing the faces of the brand assistants and brand manager and wondering, "to whom should I deliver the bad news first?" I can see my little office and the dark purple wall covering (it was the late seventies) in the hallway beyond it. I can remember wishing I were anywhere else, doing any job, as long as it wasn't that one.

My contemporary client is a wedding couple ("off the street" or "no name" in the trade) who had fallen in love with the main church interior. With some rather ardent pressure from them, we made several assumptions about when the major renovation on the church would start in the summer, and I agreed to do their wedding in June. Only now (since yesterday) it appears that the demolition of the chancel will slightly precede their nuptial date. Perhaps not, but we can't know for sure for at least a couple of weeks.

Oops. That they can use our chapel for their small wedding does not seem to diminish their disappointment and feelings of betrayal. They do not want to be mollified. I can think of any number of not-so-useful things to say, like "it's just a wedding, for crying out loud," or "if this is the worst thing you have to cope with in your marriage, consider yourselves lucky." Instead, I've assured them that their wedding will be wonderful, no matter where it takes place. While this is probably true, the whole situation brings up realities about work life I hadn't considered for a while.

Like being responsible for things over which you ultimately have no control. Having to go back on your word, especially when you have given it in good faith. Feeling that you made an error in judgment when you should have known better. Having to accept a client's or boss's wrath, no matter how reasonable or unreasonable. Come to think of it, this list pretty much summarizes my career as an advertising account executive. Ministry definitely has fewer of these hazards, or I've gotten smarter or more cautious.

I have the impression, though, that work life inevitably contains many of these ethical and organizational sand traps. As much as we may claim to believe in an all-forgiving God, the business world is not nearly so merciful. Nor, often, are our own consciences. My wedding snafu is, fortunately, a very small problem with few serious consequences (though not in the opinion of young Tim and Tara). The stakes and mistakes can call into question the integrity of an entire organization.

So there is a tension. A high-performance organization must demand excellence, even in small details. It also must remain human, so that fear and defensiveness do not drown out initiative and the willingness to make decisions. So, too, for each of us. It is okay to have high standards of performance and achievement for ourselves and for those with whom we work. For Christians, it is essential to accept ourselves and others as flawed and fallible, always falling short of perfection, but usually doing the best we can.

## *Oops*

Jesus, your disciples regularly questioned your judgment,
thought you had made mistakes,
wanted you to change strategies and stay out of trouble.
Your colleagues among the Pharisees kept trying to get you
to calm the rhetoric, follow the rules, and stay under
the political radar screen.
You didn't.
And you paid such an enormous price.
My little decisions and dilemmas are nothing like yours.
Most of the time, I do just the opposite of what you did.
I do what is expected of me, and I do it well.
I make things happen the way they are supposed to.
And I really hate it when I can't.
Help me remember, my Lord,
that being right and staying out of trouble,
receiving praise and not criticism,
not having to deliver bad news,
may make my life more comfortable
and my career more successful,
but it may not be what you most care about
from me or for me.

Lord,
when I screw up
or just plain fail,
when I am embarrassed
or feel that I should have known better,
when I make an unpopular decision
or go against the advice of others,
remind me that is when you are right there with me:
urging me
to courage of voice and conscience,
forgiveness of self and others,
and trust in your mercy and unqualified love.
Help me learn from my chagrin and self-disillusionment
to accept my own limitations.
Give me the perspective
to remember that my suffering is momentary;
that a thousand ages in your sight are like an evening gone.
This evening, help me heal and forgive,
let go of the errors of the hours past,
and embrace the peace and acceptance
you risked all
to offer to those who put their trust in you.
Amen

*       *       *

## Probability and the Holy Spirit

I've been thinking about risk and uncertainty. A University of Chicago economist named Frank Wright spelled out the difference in a famous book published in 1921 called Risk, Uncertainty, and Profit. Simply put, risk is a quantifiable calculation of expected gain or loss based on known probabilities. Uncertainty is the inability to make that calculation because the variables that determine costs and benefits are too numerous or unpredictable to be assigned a value. Markets, corporations, and economists use one concept as a tool for decision-making—risk analysis—and view the other concept—uncertainty—as a nemesis to which one must resign oneself, or overcome in a triumph of courage over evidence.

Margaret Wheatley applies theories about the natural order to organizations and human systems, and suggests that there is a self-organizing property of very complex systems—even, or especially, chaotic ones—that transcends our efforts to manage them. On her website, we read,

> *I remember the great revelatory moment I had when I was writing my first book that order and control are two different phenomena. In the Western leadership tradition, we believe that order is only available through the control we exert. But I realized that order is available through different processes that have nothing to do with our own authorship—that this world is in fact exquisitely ordered, but not necessarily for our own purposes. The Western tradition is to*

*play God with the world, assuming that nothing happens unless*
*we make it happen.*
*Leaders are so afraid of paradox, so afraid of uncertainty. It takes*
*a lot of bravery even to consider that uncertainty is not a threat,*
*that in fact it's creative and powerful.*

It's hard to believe that the international conflict and misun-
derstanding that we see nightly is moving us, unintentionally, to a
higher order of things. It may be so.

Closer to home, the circumstances in our own lives or work
that seem out of control or chaotic may really be creative moments
of transition and evolution. This view, drawn from natural science,
is consistent with what we believe about the work of the Holy
Spirit in the world. This doesn't mean we should just coast, figuring we have no control. Instead, it means acting in the most
responsible way we can today, without assuming we can or must
control the outcome. Feels like a huge leap to me.

## *Holy Spirit*

Holy Spirit,
we measure strength
by billions of dollars,
thousands of soldiers,
assets under management,
net worth,
pounds bench pressed,
proxies or protestors counted.
We think of you as
a whisper,
a wind,
a silence,
a surprise.
With the strength of water on stone,
or sunlight on ice,
crack open our resistance
and wear down our certainty
until we can trust
in your invisible
infinitesimal
yet infinite power
to create
and heal
and transform.
Amen

\*          \*          \*

## Pushing

Maybe there is such a thing as an ideal rainy weekend. We in New England recently have had several dozen to choose from. During the last one, my fourteen-year-old son miraculously began, and almost finished, a massive suburban renewal project in his room. I conducted a wedding with an outdoor reception during the one relatively dry stretch of the three days. At the wedding, I caught up with old friends who had nobly soldiered through ten years of incredibly difficult family experiences, and have emerged grateful and blessed on the other side.

My weekend reminds me how little control we have over things, and how mysterious the workings of the universe—the actions of God—really are. And it poses a faith conundrum that I don't think I'll ever resolve, at least as long as I am on this side of eternity and "seeing through a mirror dimly." Just how much do we push to change things or make things happen? How much do we "let go and let God?"

Take my son's room. Until a few days ago, it was an impassable suburban jungle, with debris of every kind in mounds on the floor. No incentives, no offers of help, no threats or commands from me had made even a dent. Then, suddenly, he decided to clean it up and reorganize it. Without my help. All he required was admiration, praise, and hints of some new furnishings, now that we can see the floor. I know part of what motivated him is simply cognitive development, moving from concrete thinking to abstract thinking, with a consequent ability to imagine and categorize. And some of it is just mystery.

I believe this tension between making things happen and letting things happen is always present in work, in organizational life, and in family life. I also believe that God will help us choose the course that is most faithful and productive if we pray constantly. God's guidance won't be in the form of a Power Point presentation. It's more like one of those kids' games where you find shapes hidden in a picture. If you get beyond the obvious, God's subtle cues—hidden in plain view—leap out at you.

## *Pushing*

In my work today, O God,
I'll make dozens of decisions.
Some are easy.
Many are driven by time pressure.
A few will have a big impact
on the futures of colleagues, subordinates, families.
The hardest part
is knowing how hard I should push.
Sometimes, I have to make others uncomfortable
in order to move us forward.
Sometimes I have to let go
and let them make a decision at their own pace.
Sometimes it feels like I have been gnawing at the same
issue forever
without getting anywhere.
Sometimes I have to do things I secretly fear,
without being sure I'm really ready,
or that anyone else is, either.

It can feel like cheating
to ask for your help.
Most of my decisions aren't that important—
I figure I should have the gumption to work them out myself.
But I know you have promised
to be a "fire by night and a cloud by day"
to all who follow you, God.
Help me get better, O God,
at asking for your guidance,
at seeing your signs,
and at trusting in your timing,
here at work today
and always.
Amen

*        *        *

## Rapid Cycling

Psychiatrists recognize a type of brain disturbance that includes
"rapid cycling" between high and low emotional states. It occurs to
me that instant communication is causing "rapid cycling" on a
mass scale. Good and bad news come hurtling at us each day,
unfiltered and unanalyzed, more times and from more directions
than we can count. It's very hard to feel that we've got our bear-
ings. Are we sad and disturbed about the consequences of war, or
relieved that "the bad guys" are losing power? Is the latest friend
or family member with cancer doing well, or poorly? Did that job
contact return our call, or did that voice mail we left get deleted?
Is our child doing well, or not? What if it all changes tomorrow,
or within the hour?

Perhaps Dickens' opening statement in his novel about the
French Revolution applies to any time of war, or to the whole of
human life: "It was the best of times, it was the worst of times."
Dickens' words point toward the variable condition of human life,
in contrast to the constant nature of God. "Change and decay in all
around I see; O, thou who changest not, abide with me." Today's
overwhelming flood of conflicting, disorienting, electronic information reminds us of this profound difference between fretful mortal
creature and calm eternal Creator, and makes us aware of our
dependence on God as source and ground of tranquility and joy.

## Rapid Cycling

O God,
the antics of a puppy
or the smile of a child
bring sudden relief,
a brief shower of joy
on a day when the winds of cyberspace
carry the sound and scent of war.
All around us creeps a fog of uncertainty
scarcely penetrated by the "facts" that are reported
hour after hour.
The fear of civilians and soldiers fills our imaginations
as surely as smoke and dust must fill their nostrils,
and impairs our ability
to perceive the goodness of creation
and the bright blessing of this day.
We are hunkered down,
but we keep peeking out of our office bunkers,
on the chance
that there might be a break in the overcast
somewhere near our mind's horizon.

Yet you, O God,
lead us unfalteringly toward Exodus and Easter.
In moments of deep need, we seize the grace you offer us
as a child takes a grownup's hand in the dark.
Sometimes we are tempted to complain

about the sustenance you provide on the way.
In our disappointment,
we yank our hand from yours
and bolt off to find something better.
Stop us, God!
Step into the centers of our lives
and bring stillness.
Slow down the rapid cycling
of our emotions and desires.
Give us the gift of calm trust in your presence
this moment, this hour,
this day,
in which a chaotic and ambiguous world
is again redeemed
by your love.
Amen

*        *        *

## Recovering Hope

My experience for many years has been that the dust-colored light and early dusk of December somehow make the pain in people's faces more visible. Perhaps it is that in a colorless time of year we see the shades of gray more clearly.

In the spring of 1999, about 90% of the managers I surveyed for my doctoral thesis agreed with the statement, "I feel hopeful about the future." I suspected then that much of their hope was grounded in an assessment of personal stability and an expectation of future earnings. It's clear that many of us have since discovered the need to find hope in something else. So it was a good reminder to me to read the conclusion of my dissertation on "Ministry to Managers in the New Corporate Era." It is more of a creed than a prayer: an affirmation of faith that I have come to experience, to believe, to proclaim, and at times, to need:

*In a lot of ways, the business world seems very different from the playground where our homeless children played, and my friend and I talked about the need for prayer in our efforts to help them and their families "make it" in the system. It's really not so different. In both worlds, the needs and the challenges come down to the same thing: to trustworthiness, to vulnerability, and to contingency [accepting uncertainty]. In a word, to covenant. In figuring out what to do in the world, whether how to house homeless families, market computers, or manage a struggling health care provider, we all need to trust and be trusted; we need to cope with our vulnerability and others', and we need to face an unknown future with confidence that we will not be abandoned.*

*That is the covenant God made with all of us. The essential
requirement of our vocation as Christians in the world and
workplace is to be faithful to that covenant, to extend our
covenantal relationships—even if temporary—to others. Such
vocation may or may not mean career success. God's covenant
with Israel did not prevent their period of slavery in Egypt, nor
did it spare Jesus from the cross. Covenant faithfulness in
business is not a lucky talisman that will bring in sure sales, but
neither is it a luxury to be thrown overboard when things get
rough and it's "everyone for himself." Covenant faithfulness—
trustworthiness, mutual care, openness to contingency, and willingness to be touched— is what makes life, including business life,
worth living: meaningful when it seems meaningless, bearable
when it seems unbearable, and joyful when moments of
achievement can be shared and celebrated.*

*God, the source of covenant faithfulness and love, is present in
every moment of creation. God chose a nomad people to be a
moral light to the nations. God chose Bethlehem and Nazareth,
two little backwater towns in a tiny has-been kingdom, to plant
the seed of God's salvation. God chose those who were poor and
uneducated to become the carriers of the Gospel. Nothing is too
trivial and no one is too insignificant to bother God about,
because God is already there. There are no elevators or
conference rooms or cubicles that are empty of God's presence.
Nothing is too worldly or powerful for God. God's faithful
presence and indestructible promise are no more stymied by the*

*creative destruction" of the economic system, or by belligerent bosses, bad quarterly results and looming deadlines, or by human theories, arrogance, or doubt than they were by the Red Sea waters or the storms of the Sea of Galilee. So the question is not really whether we can, or should pray to God about work or about homeless children. We are already in prayer: God is already listening, responding, and calling. It's just a matter of our keeping up our part of the conversation.*

## *Recovering Hope*

God of Life,
It's frightening to see grown men,
former vice presidents and
CEOs,
with tears glistening in their eyes.
It's hard to comfort a young adult
who bravely tries not to limp
from wounds to the soul
that ache at night
and come from a time
she doesn't even remember.
Then,
when it seems that the universe cannot hold
one more molecule of sadness and fear,
a tiny filament of hope catches fire:
because of some stray kindness
or accident of grace,
from some spark of empathy that arcs between two hurting souls
and burns just long enough
to let us see in the twilight
that your last and eternal word
is hope.
Amen

*          *          *

## *Repentance*

I casually flipped open my favorite devotional. The entry began, "confusion can be a gift from God." In that case, I've been exceptionally gifted this week. I have not had the energy or the will to plow through my schedule as usual.

So what has God been telling me all week? My all-too-pointed devotional reading continues,

> *When I know too much about my options before the time is right to exercise those options, I tend to use the information only to drive myself crazy. That is why, today, when I am feeling confused, I try to consider it grace. It may not yet be time for me to act.*

Or to feel 100%. Or have that resume written or proposal done, to have that definitive talk with a colleague or family member, to make that fateful decision or even to go to the grocery store. Wait? Not get it done? Trust that may not only be okay, but the waiting, inertia, and uncertainty might even be the will of God?

I'm guessing that most of us have been task- and achievement-oriented for so long, that we wouldn't recognize a fallow period if it came up and bit us. The thought of just stopping and resting, or being indecisive or undecided fills us with such guilt and fears of inadequacy that we either have to get the flu or plan an expensive vacation to be willing to do it. Some contrast to the Bedouin shepherds I remember from the desert in Israel, who, like Abraham 4,000 years before, sit all day in solitude in the wilderness, just being, not caring a whit whether it is Monday or Friday.

So here's a thought about Lent for managers: maybe it is more about doing and being less, rather than more; trusting that God not only accepts that of us; God wills it, in order to restore us to proper relationship with God and with ourselves.

## Repentance

I saw the Whirling Dervishes, God,
in a mountain town called Konya
on barren plains in Turkey.
I thought, from American cartoons,
that they would spin around in a frenzy—the managerial ideal:
to be able to go faster and faster, yet still keep your balance.
That's not what they did, God.
They spun slowly and deliberately for a long time
(till we got fidgety)
letting go of the outside world— us foreign tourist spectators—
as they centered on you.
Theirs was an Islamic mystic ritual, God,
but they spoke your Word to me:
to turn away, slowly and deliberately,
from the world that I see as my audience,
my critics,
my clients,
my responsibility,
and to focus on keeping my balance
with you.
Not because I know the goal
or can expect the answer;
but because you are the center.

For these Lenten moments, O God,
help me give up the illusion of clear direction and control,
and turn slowly in your presence:
so I may let go of the pretense and pressures
that bind me anxiously to the world,
and find release and true strength
and pure, unconditional acceptance in you,
through Christ, who shared my human frailty
and thus redeemed it. Amen

\*       \*       \*

## *Reticent Proselytes*

Here's the question we stumbled on at our downtown lunch gathering: Do you have a Bible at work? Only one person did. Would you take a Bible to work? Why or why not? Where do you put it? How would you feel about someone at work seeing you read it? Under what circumstances might you open it?

Turns out, to no one's surprise, people were more anxious about being thought to be proselytizing than enthusiastic about having the written Word of God handy. This may have something to do with some folks finding the Bible a rather intimidating, opaque book, hard to navigate in a moment of need. We agreed to address that problem by coming up with a business person's bookmark, containing passages useful in a variety of circumstances. It remains to be seen how many Bibles will find their way into desk drawers or onto desk tops as a result of our conversation. On the other hand, this may be an outmoded issue. We know a seminarian who has the Bible programmed into his Palm Pilot, and anyone can find the passage of his choice at www.bible.com.

Many of us, fearful of being pushy, offensive, or (worse yet) viewed as "too religious," keep silent on the subject of our faith, especially at work. We may believe (appropriately) that the way we behave and treat others is a testimony to our belief. Our works are important. Words matter, too. Even if we are not ready to share them out loud with others in the workplace, it is important to pray and read them for ourselves. Even at work. So, think about what it would mean to have a Bible at work. Or at least put www.bible.com on your favorites list.

## *Reticent Proselytes*

God,
I do not speak your name in meetings
(except as a mild expletive)
and I confess that I often forget to pray at work.
It's not clear to me how the ancient words and situations
of the Bible
would be relevant to daily hassles in my office,
or helpful when I'm at a loss or facing a decision.
I might forget to read a Bible even if I had one here.
What if I took a chance?
What if I read a psalm when I ate lunch at my desk?
What if I remembered, and pulled my Bible, along with my Advil,
out of my desk when I was stuck or angry?
What if someone saw me reading it,
and asked me a question about my faith?
Would it be so awful if I got caught?
Help me think and pray about this, God.
Give me the courage and the wisdom
to accept your Word of scripture, even at work.
Give me the eyes of faith to discern
as Jesus did again and again,
the moments when someone I meet
might need to hear your good news from me.
I pray this in the name of the Risen Christ,
who commanded Peter to feed his lambs,
and commands that of each of us, too.
Amen

\*     \*     \*

## Special or Not

A good friend gave me a Mighty Mouse "wacky wobbler" figure for my birthday. It is the perfect gift. Mighty Mouse was THE cartoon character of my childhood. (When I was four, we played "Mighty Mouse" in the neighborhood. I am embarrassed to report that I always got to be Mighty Mouse.) For many years of adulthood, MM has been the defining symbol of my personality—and personality flaws. The best (and most therapeutic) thing about this Mighty Mouse doll is that however you bounce his head, he shakes it in an emphatic "NO." I should get the hint.

Contemplating my birthday and Mighty Mouse, it occurs to me that there are two ways to feel special: one is to accomplish great things and be praised for them, another is to be cared for with genuine, disinterested tenderness and love. I suppose a perfect life (whatever that is) would include both experiences in great abundance.

I suspect, however, that I am not the only highly responsible, upwardly mobile child of the 1950s and 60s to have grown up with a rather lopsided set of accounts in the "specialness" department. When a B+ is considered failure it's pretty clear that there's no such thing as being accepted just for who you are. Organizational life, at the rarified levels we in the "professional class" live it, puts a very clear emphasis on achievement as a source of reward, appreciation, and dignity. Even in an occupation focused on "loving one another" I spend an absurdly large amount of my time trying to save the day, or to run faster, think smarter, write better for some imaginary audience. On a daily basis, I am more worried about not being "as good as" or "better than" than I am about being struck by a car or some dread disease. As my son would say, "that is SAD."

In more inspired moments, I remember that Jesus doesn't care a whit about all the starring roles I have managed to land in the past, or contemplate in the future. Jesus sees the entire backstage area of my life, even my chaotic closets, and loves me. Jesus wants me to sleep restfully, and awaken with joy, no matter what is left undone, or doesn't quite work out. Imagine that!

## Special or Not

Jesus,
what is it like to watch me
and all the others like me,
who start our mornings with caffeine and workouts
so we can be razor sharp and on the ball
all day long?
What do you do
when you see our shoulders tense
and our stomachs tighten
because we've forgotten a deadline,
or failed to live up to expectations—
our own, or someone else's?
What are your expectations, Jesus?
Do they have anything to do
with desks, computers, and conference calls?
Do you want us to work harder, faster, better
to save the day? To save the world? To save our jobs?
Or have I got it backwards ...
could you want to take care of me,
and lighten my burdens,
rather than judge how much I can carry?
Is it possible that you think I am special
just because you made me
and gave me a unique way of loving you?
Help me accept my flaws and limitations.

Remind me
that you are wiser and more knowing than
my boss, my professor, my mother, or my superego,
and that you love me just as I am,
with my superhero cloak chucked in the closet
and my "to do" list still undone.
Amen

*     *     *

## Thanksgiving for Bits of Grace

I found myself muttering this morning, "You know God, I'm really tired of dealing with this." Then it occurred to me, in a blinding flash of insight, that life is a chronic condition. Practically everyone I know lives with some kind of intractable problem, whether physical, medical, spiritual, financial, relational, occupational, emotional, legal, or all of the above. And we all live with the chronic conditions of sin and mortality. Am I entitled to complain? Well, yes. So are we all. So was the psalmist. For the psalmist, sometimes not even prayer seemed to help. We can relate, right?

*Psalm 77*

*I cry aloud to God,*
*aloud to God that he may hear me.*
*In the day of my trouble I seek the Lord;*
*in the night my hand is stretched out without wearying;*
*my soul refuses to be comforted.*
*I think of God, and I moan;*
*I meditate, and my spirit faints. (1—3)*

He even wonders,

*Has God forgotten to be gracious?*
*Has he in anger shut up his compassion? (9)*

Then, recollecting himself, he affirms his faith in God's past mercy:

*I will call to mind the deeds of the Lord;*
*I will remember your wonders of old.*
*I will meditate on all your work,*
*and muse on your mighty deeds.*
*With your strong arm you redeemed your people,*
*the descendants of Jacob and Joseph. (11, 12, 15)*

The Psalmist reminds himself of God's miraculous power over creation:

*When the waters saw you, they were afraid,*
*the very deep trembled.*
*Your way was through the sea,*
*your path, through the mighty waters;*
*yet your footprints were unseen. (16, 19)*

Biblical faith starts where we are right now, no matter how miserable or unpromising that place may seem. It invites us to draw strength and hope from the history of God's loving care for God's people, and from the miracle of creation itself. I haven't worked out my intransigent issues since this morning. I did go for a walk with my dogs. The early spring sky was so blue, the air so fresh, it was almost intoxicating.

My favorite tree—a huge oak at the end of our walk—is starting to bud. It was an hour filled with much-needed grace. I was reminded again of this past Sunday's epistle reading:

*God is faithful, and he will not let you be tested beyond your strength, but with the testing he will also provide the way out so that you may be able to endure it. (1 Corinthians 10:13)*

## *Thanksgiving for Bits of Grace*

Okay, God,
I guess you're not going to part the sea
and get me out of this place.
Even if you did, I'd still have the desert in front of me.
So thank you for the bits of grace that float past me,
inviting me to lift my hands and spirit and grab hold,
if only for a moment.
Thank you for the spring sun,
which works its miracle of restoration
as surely on suburbanites today
as it did on shepherds of ages past.
Thank you for listening to my complaints
and suffering beside me, silent but present, in my loneliest hours.
Thank you for giving me the strength not to give up.
Thank you for occasionally showing my human and animal
companions just what I need.
Thank you for my life,
and the freedom to create something new with it, even if it's tiny,
every day.
Thank you for staying here with me,
and for helping me see, in the rich history of your merciful acts,
not just the solution to my problems,
but no less than the promise of my salvation
and the salvation of the world,
through Jesus who suffered and redeemed us all.
Amen

*          *          *

## Thanksgiving for Joy in Work

I recently wrote a prayer for our high school students facing final exams. It got me to pondering whether it's better to have finals at the end of a term (which I always dreaded) or to have rolling "finals" throughout the year, which is, I believe, what work life is like. Instead of "world without end" it's "exams without end."

I guess I'm happier with this arrangement than I would like to admit, because many of the deadlines, projects and responsibilities that count as my "exams" are almost entirely self-inflicted, or to put it more positively, "self-initiated." Turns out, part of the fun—the challenge and the adrenaline rush—of work is to figure out new ways to do things, and new things to do, to further the mission of the organization.

Ah, but there are many caveats that come with this entrepreneurial approach to work. Like, don't neglect the basics: mere innovation isn't enough. Beware of becoming an urgency addict: someone who always has too much to do, so whatever you're finally (belatedly) working on is always marked "urgent."

There is also joy, pride, and satisfaction from doing good work in the world, and that is reason to celebrate.

## *Thanksgiving for Joy in Work*

Thank you, God,
for giving me work to do.
Thank you for the easy things:
the needs and questions that,
because of my experience and networks and know-how,
I can respond to with a minimum of difficulty,
and a maximum of good effect.
Thank you for the hard things:
the crises that push me to think hard and fast,
dig deeply,
engage others,
and reach out to you
to make things come out okay.
Thank you for the people I can count on
to seize upon an imaginative idea and keep it afloat.
And thank you—really—
for those I can count on
to point out the holes in the idea,
and to "reality test" my creations.
I know I need them, too.

Thank you, God,
for the quirky things that happen at work
and make me part of a sometimes crazy family,
a community
that has a shared history,
unique rituals,
unspoken understandings,
and moments of good will and grace,
all of which remind me
that being human
and being at work
can be one and the same.
Amen

\*          \*          \*

## *Thanksgiving for Those I Meet*

The renovation of our worship space last summer included major changes in seating. In the congregation, the new pews are curved in a semi-circle. Our choir, which is in the front of the church, now faces the congregation in a semi-circle. In the previous layout, the choir was divided on two sides of the chancel, facing toward each other, and perpendicular to the congregation. So only those at the front of the choir could see or be seen by the congregation. These changes are great acoustically, and allow both choir and congregation to share an aspect of worship that I have long treasured. They are able to see one another. I consider this a great spiritual opportunity.

It goes back to when I was in high school in a tiny Episcopal mission parish on a university campus. The congregation was small but diverse. The chapel was modern, with tall white brick walls and triangular sky lights in the roof that formed prisms in an ever-changing pattern on the interior surfaces. Even on the darkest day, I found it an airy and inspiring space. The last six rows of pews rose steeply to form a choir loft. I was part of a tiny high school choir.

The moment I'll never forget occurred one day in late winter. It was probably Lent. I was kneeling in one of the rear pews during the communion prayer and suddenly noticed the light illuminating the people scattered in the pews below me. My eyes were drawn to their faces. It was as if Jesus himself were showing them to me. I could see the weariness, the vulnerability, the self-containment, the beauty in each middle-aged, lined, ordinary face. I was filled with awe and tenderness at the recognition of their need and humanity, and their preciousness to Christ. I watched them as they went forward for communion and returned, somehow filled, and then knelt in private communion with God. It was as if Christ taught me, in that hour, to see what he saw in them: beneath and beyond their worldly success or failure, their annoying personalities and pretensions, their strident politics or intellectual airs, their infinite value and need for love and redemption.

Fast forward thirty years. In my front row seat in the old chancel, I was privileged to see other faces in the same light each week. While I occasionally contemplated the figure of Jesus carrying the lost lamb in the Good Shepherd window at the rear of the church, more often I watched the faces of those at worship.

It was like a long silent prayer. I remembered their losses, especially the deaths of those they have loved; I wondered about the vicissitudes they face in their jobs; I thought about their struggles with depression or other emotional battles. I wondered what challenges confronted those who seem, to the world's eye, so together and successful. I saw the tenderness in the faces of new parents holding their infants. I saw the loving-but-embarrassed exasperation of parents with wiggling children, and remembered my mom telling my sister and me to sit still, with a look intended to freeze us on the spot. I would see the need, the hope, the yearning for divine connection and blessing. While there are vast differences in financial circumstances in our congregation, that hour reduces us all to our essence: people who need Christ's love and community.

This consciousness of people's essential vulnerability is what gets me through the week. I can accept (well, deal with) all kinds of flaws, idiosyncrasies, and actions that might otherwise drive me crazy, if I remember to look in their faces and see in them mystery and value. Each person looking for a food gift certificate, each nursery school mom with a monster SUV parked in my driveway, each checkout clerk or fellow languisher in a waiting room has a story only God knows. All have hurts and wisdom that give them unique roles in God's plan for salvation.

I'm glad our new worship space allows others to share this precious gift of sight that Christ gives. And I'm grateful that Christ renews and offers this gift to each of us who worship together every Sunday.

## Thanksgiving for Those I Meet

Loving Jesus,
In your time on earth,
you saw the truth in the face of each person you met.
Whether great or small,
whatever their station or their past,
you saw their faith, their desperation, their hope,
their hardness of heart,
their need for redemption and healing.
Thank you for the privilege
of sharing, in some small measure,
this truth which the Holy Spirit reveals
to all who love and follow you.
Thank you, for stepping in front of me when I'm in the midst of
pique and irritation,
placing your fingers on my lips,
so that silenced, I may follow your gaze,
and see the vulnerability and humanity
of those who annoy me,
who disagree with me,
who are hopelessly slow,
or seem just plain evil.
Thank you for reminding me
that my gift of sight is only partial
and that I can trust you to know
and judge with equity
those whom I might be tempted to despise.

Thank you, for standing by my side
and pointing out, when I least expect it
in a meeting, an elevator, a waiting room or classroom,
the beauty and mystery of ordinary faces.
Thank you for nudging me to wonder about their stories,
their hurts and hopes and disappointments,
the truth about life that they can reveal to me
if I pay close attention to you, and to them.
Thank you, for making some of those faces
familiar and precious to me as they are to you,
yet still filled with mystery and promise waiting to be revealed;
in the place where I work,
in the place I call home,
and especially in your holy mystery, the church,
where earthly hope and sorrow
and heaven meet
in the faces of those who gather
to worship you.
Amen

*       *       *

## Thanksgiving in All Circumstances

At the end of Paul's first letter to the Thessalonians there are a series of exhortations that are often used at the close of worship.

> *...encourage the faint hearted, help the weak, be patient with all of them. See that none of you repays evil with evil, but always seek to do good to one another and to all. Rejoice always, pray without ceasing, give thanks in all circumstances. ... Hold fast to what is good; abstain from every form of evil. ..."*
>
> *(1 Thessalonians 5:14—22)*

The words that have been on my mind are "rejoice always ... give thanks in all circumstances ... hold fast to what is good." This past week some very good and some very sad things have swept my attention away from my usual preoccupations. The good, certainly small by world standards, is that our son made middle school jazz band as a trumpet player. He worked very hard for this. It was his first foray into competition for a coveted position among his peers. While I was prepared (sort of) for a hard life lesson in surviving failure, I was infinitely relieved that we were able to savor this moment of success and satisfaction.

We had just gotten back from a small celebratory dinner when the call came that our former church moderator and loved and admired patriarch had just died. At age 79, he had had numerous health problems, but his death seemed very sudden. His funeral will be the hardest in a long time.

So I am trying very hard to "hold fast to what is good." I am puzzled and disoriented by this very commonplace collision of good and bad news. These things aren't additive. You can't sum them and get a level of "net happiness" or "net sadness." They coexist awkwardly, jostling for position in one's consciousness and wrestling in one's sleep. It is possible to be happy and sad at the same time, to both grieve and rejoice. Paul reminds us that no matter what, we have reason to give thanks.

## Thanksgiving in All Circumstances

I thank you, God,
for the intertwined gifts of feeling true joy and true sadness
on behalf of another human being.
I thank you that others touch me so deeply
that I am moved to delight and to tears.
I thank you that you offer your loving care
in times of sorrow and in times of success.
I thank you for good things that make me smile with others
and for the consoling truth of our funeral prayer:
*"We thank you especially that in the night of our grief*
*and in the shadows of our sorrow,*
*we are not left to ourselves.*
*We have the light of your promises*
*to sustain and comfort us."*
I thank you that my deepest darkness is not dark to you, O God,
and that you hold hope in your hand
when it is completely beyond my sight.
I thank you that the evils and injustices of the world,
which so easily overwhelm me,
are not proof against your goodness,
nor can they endure in the face of your love.
I thank you for giving me the courage
to hold fast to what is good,
trusting that you will reveal to the eyes of faith
the source of true joy:
the saving grace of Jesus Christ, our Lord.
Amen

*          *          *

## Untying Knots

I should have known it was Oscar Wilde. "The truth is rarely pure
and never simple." If we could all just remember that. The way
one of my psychology professors put it was, "everyone acts in a
way that seems reasonable to him." Even folks whose choices and
behavior are incomprehensible to me. In any situation each of us
holds onto our truth, our view of the facts, our beliefs about what
is reasonable, our account of who did what to whom, and what
should be done about it, with tenacity and with the conviction we
are right, and surely justified by morality, experience, or pragma-
tism.

I've watched many examples of this seemingly inevitable
human behavior—and source of conflict. They often involve so
much pain, and the stakes are often high: the survival of families,
businesses, and relationships. The higher the stakes, the more desperately we cling to the truth as we understand it. Even when the
issues aren't ultimate, attitudes can become rigid, and resolution
impossible.

Cicero was said to be an unsuccessful politician because he
was too willing to look at an issue from all sides. Perhaps such a
stance is bad for a political career. However, "multidirectional par-
tiality," a willingness to consider every side with empathy, is a
good thing for most of the rest of us to cultivate. Jesus was especially good at doing this: having compassion and respect for each
person he encountered. I think trying to do that even when we
don't feel like it helps the church become the church, and makes
us disciples and evangelists for Christ in the workplace and community, even if we never utter his name.

## Untying Knots

God,
every child knows
that Mom can untie any knot
in shoelaces or Christmas tree lights
or in a piece of rope or string,
even after we've pulled and tugged on it,
and it's just gotten tighter
as we got more frustrated.
We know how Mom does it.
She patiently finds the ends tangled in the mess
and traces where they go.
She loosens the tension on the knot,
and patiently works on the edges of the knot
with her fingers.
Or she finds something sharp
that can get into the center
and open up some space
where we pulled the knot tightest.
When we grow up,
we forget that you do the same thing for us,
if we ask.

When we are angry
or hurt about something someone has done,
or see things differently
and come to conflicting conclusions or differing solutions,
we often just pull harder on our end
and the knot becomes tighter,
till we can't untangle it
or our feelings,
or undo the harm we have done.
Remind us, loving God
when we start to feel tense or angry, hurt or afraid
or frustrated by some intransigent foe (or fool)
to let go and hand the knot to you.
To remember that we can't see through
the tangles of human feelings
or pick apart multiple truths
but you can.
And if we accept that neither we
nor others possess the whole of your truth,
and can relax just enough
and wait to let your Spirit move,
you will hand the string back to us, unknotted,
and we will ask
like we did when we were kids,
"How did you do that?"
Amen

\*         \*         \*

## When New Responsibilities Loom

It was my first personal election-eve since high school. Back then, I was considered too intellectual and insufficiently flamboyant to be electable—the Al Gore problem, I guess—but this time there were numerous signs that I would be elected to the Board of Commissioners for the Wellesley Housing Authority. So my answer, when people asked me, "Are you worried about the election?" was no—not about the election. It was what might come after the election that spiked my anxiety. It wasn't the extra time commitment; juggling my schedule long ago became a way of life. It was the new and possibly inflated expectations—my own and others'—that gave me pause.

In the midst of the pre-election angst, a wise friend sent me a book for our church library. It's called Quotes for the Journey/Wisdom for the Way compiled by Gordon S. Jackson. One quotation in the section on "busyness" was especially helpful:

> *Remember that it was God who decided on a twenty-four hour day, and he must have felt that it was enough. We can never do all that we expect ourselves to do, and can rarely do all that others expect us to do, but we can always do all that God expects us to do. (Scott Sernau)*

As God was present to Abraham and Moses and Paul, God is with us when we feel daunted by the challenges and expectations that lie ahead.

## *When New Responsibilities Loom*

God,
Help me stay calm and focused
on the work you would have me do.
Help me be a good steward of my own energy and endurance.
Let me be neither stingy nor profligate
with my effort and my commitment;
always mindful of my finite limits,
yet trustful of your infinite grace.
Help me keep the expectations and suggestions of others
in perspective,
accepting the wisdom that comes from differing points of view,
yet being faithful to your call, and to my own sense of integrity.
Make me humble enough to be flexible and willing to learn,
but courageous enough to take unpopular stands
or set limits to protect myself and those I love.
Give me the freedom to let go, to take a nap,
or even let someone down, without feeling I have failed you.
Most of all, loving God,
give me a sense of your presence with me
in the work you call me to do.
In your mercy, grant me untroubled rest at night,
confident that you accept my daily offering of myself,
not because my work is perfect, but because your love is perfect
and redeems all who place their trust in you.
Amen

*          *          *

## Would-be Believers

I felt the quivering vibrations of our confirmation class as they rehearsed for the Rite of Confirmation the following Sunday. Their anxiety was not about where they would sit and when they should stand, but other, larger issues. "How do I know what to believe?" "Why this religion instead of another?" "I still don't know enough about God to promise I'll follow God for the rest of my life."

Their honest doubt is both moving and disarming. It doesn't seem to help much to say, "Welcome to the club. We all have doubts." I don't think the confirmands are looking for empathy. They are hoping the minister can offer them some certainty. Little do they know that faith is a question of getting used to the uncertainty, rather than getting past it. They may suspect, but may not want to believe, that we adults espouse this stuff because we are more in need of imaginary crutches than they are. They are certainly deaf to the answer, "As you get older, good and bad things will happen, and people will touch you in ways that will help you experience God." This may be true, but it sounds patronizing and the kids know it does not come with a money-back guarantee.

So my prayer is for our confirmation class, and all the other fifteen-year-olds or fifty-year-olds who struggle with belief, doubt, and making promises to God.

## *Would-be Believers*

Thank God that you are God,
O God.
That spreading faith
depends on your gift of grace
and not on my sporadic and self-conscious efforts to share it.
When I am honest, God,
I admit that truth is always
just beyond the horizon of my knowing.
Sometimes I feel just on the edge of it,
sure of myself and my belief,
and then it slips away and I am aware of my confusion
and of the fleetingness of my claim to know and understand.
It's like that with people and relationships,
love and parenting,
organizations and the economy,
the stock market,
and most of all, you.
I am blessed, God.
You have revealed your love to me
in unexpected times and places,
through people who surprised and changed and comforted me,
through experiences that wounded and challenged and healed me.
When I have stumbled in doubt and darkness
you have steadily reclaimed and redirected me
and rekindled my hope.

The mounting years that have blurred my vision
and dulled my memory
have given me a consoling gift:
to realize that trust in you,
and not truth about you (or anything else)
will sustain me from this day to the next.
Help me hold this precious gift with open hands, O God,
neither greedily grasping it for myself
nor smugly shoving it at others,
but constantly aware of this blessed burden,
and trusting that you, in your time
and with your perfect knowing,
will move me to share it with others whom
you, not I, have prepared to receive it.
Amen

\*          \*          \*

# Part Four

*Seasons and Celebrations*

# WINTER PRAYERS

---

## *Thanksgiving Prayer*

O God,
whose love is not limited by time or distance or life or death,
we thank you for your presence among us here in this house,
and in all our days.
We thank you for the gift of Jesus Christ,
whom you sent to reveal to us the path
to full humanity,
and to reconciliation with you
and all our human kin.

We are so aware, O God,
in this week of Thanksgiving
of those who give thanks at tables
where a cherished voice is silent,
a beloved place is empty.
Help us support those who grieve,
help us sing your praises
even with voices choked with tears.

We are so aware, O God, in this week of family gatherings,
that many Americans across the globe
will spend Thanksgiving
putting themselves in harm's way to protect our safety.

Remind us to include in our Thanksgiving grace,
prayers for those who serve.
We are also aware, O God,
in this week when we give thanks for the blessings
you have given us,
that you are the same God
who weeps with mothers of enemy soldiers
whose lives have been lost,
who is stirred to anger at starvation
caused by human war and neglect,
who promises to judge all nations of the world
with your righteousness and truth.
Make us humbly aware, O God, in this week of harvest festival, of
Christ's command to share the feast:
with those who are alone or afraid;
with those who hunger for food or companionship;
with those who are our enemies
yet are loved and forgiven by you,
just as we have been.
Praise to you, O God,
whose goodness brings forth the fruit of the earth,
and whose mercy and righteousness endure forever.
Amen

*         *         *

## *December Prayer*

Dear Lord,
You must not know whether to laugh or cry in December.
We can be at our best or our most petty,
our most generous and our most self-absorbed.
We can be filled with hope or filled with tension
all in the same day, if not in the same hour.
We take turns pitying the less fortunate and pitying ourselves
and often miss the mark of true compassion,
either for the stranger or for our own aching hearts.
Then there are the moments of grace
when we get it right,
when we have a truly mature moment of wisdom and forbearance,
or a truly child-like moment of joy.
Help us to savor those holy moments
and to forgive ourselves and others for everything else.
Surprise us this Christmas with one, tiny gift of grace,
hidden away where we least expect it,
just as you did 2000 years ago.
Amen

\*          \*          \*

## *Advent I*

In these latter days, O God,
we've discovered
that Newton was not quite right.
Our world is not a predictable order,
governed by laws of reason and intellect.
We are endlessly surprised and baffled
by unexpected heartache and unforeseen joy,
by new possibilities that scare us no matter whether they
portend hope or harm.
In the midst of it all,
in the kaleidoscope of grief and loss,
fascination and challenge that is our lives,
we come to you.
We come to Advent,
that most vulnerable of seasons,
when the distance between the purity of your peace and love
and the ragged state of our decisions, desires, and understanding
is mostly clearly, painfully evident to us.
We can't shorten that distance by ourselves, O God.
On our own we would never get to Bethlehem,
no matter how many packages we wrap or year-end deals we
wrap up.

In fact, we don't really know how to start
to purify our lives so that we are worthy to present ourselves
to the holy Babe,
the returning King of Glory,
let alone to bind up your broken and bleeding human family
so all may join in the feast.
Help us, O God:
unsettle us enough this week
to jog us out of our predictable attitudes and answers,
our fixed beliefs about what we need to have, or do, or gain
to be happy, successful, or content.
Hold us in your mercy,
even as you refine and test us.
Transform us through your divine chemistry
to be the people you created in your image:
ministers of your grace
in the mission fields of our lives,
where you call us
to seek and share redemption
and discover your truth and joy.
Amen

*       *       *

## *Advent II*

I pray, O Holy One,
that you will use the empty space
I sometimes feel
as the holidays swirl like wind around me
to plant some new and wild hope in my heart.
Even if all I can feel now
is the pain of tilling the soil of my life,
breaking up the clods of habit and routine
which I cling to,
even when they are held together only by the entrapping roots
of smothering weeds.
Even with that pain,
I trust you to bring something wonderful into the world,
into my life,
in this season of holy birth.
I bring you the gift of my emptiness,
my need for your love,
my longing for your wholeness,
my hope for your simple joy
and merciful righteousness,
in these days of darkness
that only you can turn to light.
Amen

\*          \*          \*

## *Advent III*

This is a prayer from Advent III in December, 1990, when we sang Handel's Utrecht Te Deum, written in 1713. In 1713, England was weary and desolate from seven decades of internal conflict over religion and the control of the monarchy, and years of war with Spain and France. In 1990 American soldiers were in the Middle East fighting in the first Gulf War. In the early twenty-first century, our soldiers are again fighting in the Gulf.

Our longings for peace and hope this season have been felt by people of faith through the centuries—in fact, by the people of Israel 2000 years ago.

## *Advent III*

Gracious God, Love Divine,
How we need to hear the songs of angels.
Handel must have known that, Lord.
From the centuries, he has given us the angel songs of
"Holy, holy, holy, Lord God of Sabaoth."
We thank you for the gift of angel songs in our midst.
How we need to hear the songs of angels, Lord.
No matter how rational and grown-up we try to be,
this season undoes us.
In the very moment of your coming,
we feel vulnerable and unprepared,
and sometimes just plain scared.
We ache for soldiers half a world away,
trying to remember the songs of angels
and the smells of home.
We ache for children with too little to eat,
with cold and bleak homes
or no home at all,
whether they live six miles away,
or on the other side of the globe.
We ache for friends and family members who struggle
with loss or sickness or grief.
We ache with our own private sorrows that only you know.
Yet in this bleak mid-winter, you call us to rejoice.
We hear again the angel song:
God is with us, peace on earth, good will to all.

Help us to hear your angel voices in the days ahead, Lord.
Still our restlessness, deepen our yearning.
Train our ears and our hearts to hear the sound of your coming,
to know your joy that transcends
all earthly pain and all earthly glory.
Amen

*          *          *

## Advent IV

Ah, Lord God,
How we long to lose ourselves in the glorious music
of Christmas ...
to let go, for a moment, of the cares that cling to us.
How we thrill to the sounds of carols and glorias—
that express, not so much the gaiety we feel,
but the joy we need.
How our hearts ache for the peace that the angels sing—
peace that the world still yearns to find.
Why is it, O God, that even into this season of joy and expectation
there steals a note of sadness?
The carols that touch us most deeply are the ones that soar with
thrilling but yearning melodies.
Remind us again, and again, Our Heavenly God,
that you came to us
not to bless perfect lives or reign over perfect holidays,
but to be the presence of love and hope
in very imperfect ones.
Remind us again and again, O God,
that you came to us
not as a conquering hero scattering our enemies,
not as a jester spreading mirth,
but as the child of a poor and tired mother,
far from the home and family she knew,
deeply in need of solace and strength,
and finding it in you.

Remind us again and again
that the joy and peace we seek in the carols sung at your birth
are to be found when we let you into our lives
and welcome you into our homes.
Amen

\*        \*        \*

## *O Holy Night*

I think the carol that may best express the emotional truth of this month of longing and hope is O Holy Night. I can hear the chords as my fingers move over an imagined piano, and feel the words of the hymn sung with haunting beauty by our tenor soloist just before the start of the late service on Christmas Eve.

The music starts with a quiet affirmation of faith, in a major key.

> *O Holy Night! The stars are brightly shining,*
> *It is the night of the dear Savior's birth;*

The melody starts to repeat, but then shifts and intensifies into a minor key at the words, "till he appeared and the soul felt its worth."   At the word "felt," there is a dissonance that is resolved with the word "worth."

> *Long lay the world in sin and error pining*
> *Till He appeared and the soul felt its worth.*

Then the intensity of the words and the urgency of the chord progressions build:

> *A thrill of hope*
> *the weary world rejoices,*
> *For yonder breaks*
> *a new and glorious morn;*

At the climax of the carol, the melody and words burst into a heartfelt imperative, accompanied by rippling minor chords.

> *Fall on your knees,*
> *oh, hear the angel voices!*

Finally, the melody and chords resolve into a powerful, emotional acclamation:

> *O night divine, O night when Christ was born!*
> *O night divine, O holy night divine!*

For many of us, the moods and realities of Advent alternate between quiet moments of trusting faith and painful moments of urgent hope and yearning, tinged with unmet needs and sorrow. In the end, we reach toward hope, mysterious, divine hope, filling the night.

## O Holy Night

There is a magnifying glass of emotional truth,
O God,
that concentrates the light of hope and the heat of pain
almost to combustion
in December.
We think we are just going through the day—
in the office,
the supermarket,
at a meeting,
a rehearsal,
on the phone,
and suddenly feelings blaze up,
hope, despair and memory,
that we had forgotten
or never even knew we felt.
We are stunned,
we stagger.
The last thing we believe
is that we have any control over
this intrusion, this heart invasion.
We try to figure it out.
We measure out the distance
between our grief and imperfection
and some ideal,
not sure whether it is the grief, the ideal, or the gulf between
that has caused the pain.

The magnifying glass has a different purpose,
doesn't it, God?
It makes visible that tiny hidden spot in our lives
where your incarnate love is most needed;
it reveals a speck on the globe
that cries for our prayer
and yearns for the birth of peace.
It helps us feel
a thrill of hope
as the weary world rejoices,
for yonder breaks
a new and glorious morn.
Amen

\*      \*      \*

## *After Christmas*

"Liminal" is a great word. It comes from the Latin "threshold" and means "at a point where one perception or condition blends or crosses over into another." This is a liminal time—when with reluctance and relief, we are on the edge between sacred and ordinary time.

The poetry of "The Night Before Christmas" has been replaced by stacks of empty boxes, wrapping paper saved (maybe) for another year, gifts we don't have a place or a use for still on coffee tables, and refrigerators filled with food we don't need.

Yet we're not quite ready to go back to work, to let go of this time when we celebrate our midnights with singing, our mornings with gifts and leisurely breakfasts, and happily set aside school and train schedules.

As we step over the threshold, we wonder what will linger from these fleeting yet special moments?

## *After Christmas*

I know that going back to work, O God,
means being hard-edged and alert.
Let me take with me fresh memories
of those drowsy mystical moments
of candles and carols,
when the holy seems to blanket the earth
with hope and the promise of peace.
The day-to-day realities of budgets
and year-end results,
economic uncertainty
and fear of war
threaten to drain that promise of its power,
O God.
We go back to being fallen
and captive to worldly concerns
more quickly than we were lifted and redeemed
by the miraculous story of your birth.
Even the carols we love have become repetitious,
and the decorations that were so festive
a week ago seem a little stale.
Give us one thing to cling to, O God,
in the ordinary time to come:
that you came into the world
not to condemn us, but to share our common lot—
even in offices and supermarkets—
and to infuse these ordinary days and moments

with sacred hope and purpose.
Remind us, not only to love one another,
but to know that we ourselves,
reluctantly leaving the manger
and silencing angel glories for another year,
are daily held and cherished by you.
Amen

\*     \*     \*

## *New Year's Day*

Touch us with your hope and promise, O God,
as we pause at the changing of the year.
Forgive us those things of the year past
we wish we could do differently:
words we should have left unspoken,
actions we did not have the courage to take.
Remind us, in this moment of awareness,
that each day is a new beginning
in Christ.
Fill us with your Holy Spirit
so we may enter this new year
with cleansed and penitent hearts,
confident of your love and care for us,
guided by your justice and righteousness,
and filled with zeal
to accomplish your will for our lives
in our daily work and worship.
Amen

\*          \*          \*

# SPRING/SUMMER PRAYERS

## Lent

The English detective-novel-on-tape to which I am currently
addicted served up today the only bit of poetry I have ever unintentionally memorized: "Things fall apart, the center cannot
hold/Mere anarchy is loosed upon the world." It wasn't completely accidental. I agonized over the entire poem for an all-night college English paper that made me swear off Yeats forever. That line
must have stuck for a reason, however, and struck me today
because it describes the current state of the inside of my head, the
surface of my desk, and the state of the world where things near
and far away seem beyond redemption. Though the poem has a
distinctly anti-religious strain, its description of the current human
situation is chillingly apropos, as armored tanks rumble throughout
the Middle East.

### The Second Coming
*Turning and turning in the widening gyre*
*The falcon cannot hear the falconer;*
*Things fall apart; the centre cannot hold;*
*Mere anarchy is loosed upon the world,*
*The blood-dimmed tide is loosed, and everywhere*
*The ceremony of innocence is drowned;*
*The best lack all conviction, while the worst*
*Are full of passionate intensity.*

*Surely some revelation is at hand;*
*Surely the Second Coming is at hand.*
*The Second Coming! Hardly are those words out*
*When a vast image out of Spiritus Mundi*
*Troubles my sight: somewhere in the sands of the desert*
*A shape with lion body and the head of a man,*
*A gaze blank and pitiless as the sun,*
*Is moving its slow thighs, while all about it*
*Reel shadows of the indignant desert birds.*
*The darkness drops again; but now I know*
*That twenty centuries of stony sleep*
*Were vexed to nightmare by a rocking cradle,*
*And what rough beast, its hour come round at last,*
*Slouches towards Bethlehem to be born?*

*(W. B. Yeats)*

The events of the world and our powerlessness to alter them can lead to a profound sense of despair. It makes me wonder how Jesus felt as he walked up the dusty road from Jericho to Jerusalem the last time. Was he exhausted? Did his back and neck ache from the tension of holding in all that he had yet to face? Did he feel distanced even from those who were closest to him, and from the crowds who lined the road, who expected something more and different from him than he could possibly provide? Probably. Did he really understand what God had in mind for him? Probably not.

It's okay to be in a bad place for a while. Elijah was there. So were David, Paul, and even Jesus. Unlike Mr. Yeats, we who struggle to follow Jesus—however nightmarish our collective efforts have sometimes been over the centuries—don't conclude that the spiritual desert is where we end up.

## Lent

Jesus,
Help me see resurrection
in a world that seems stalled in Passiontide.
My little hurts and worries
hardly seem worthy of a sign of resurrection power,
even though they are sometimes more than I can bear.
The great sorrows,
the impossible tragedy of Israelis and Palestinians,
the citizens lost in the endless maze of violence
in Liberia or Uganda,
the families who sit waiting in agony in hospital rooms
and court rooms in every county in the country,
how does resurrection come to them?
I know I cannot know the answer.
But I trust you have already answered
each ugly snarl
or terrifying whisper
of death and sin,
violence and fear
with love that is stronger, lasts longer,
and is more patient than despair.
I also know that sometime today or tomorrow,
or maybe the day after that,
or perhaps next week,

I will stumble upon something
luminous and wonderful,
even if just for a minute,
that will warm me or make me smile
or fill me with comfort or hope,
and I will know you have not abandoned us,
that the Easter power of resurrection will not cease
to move upon the earth
until the whole creation is redeemed.
Amen

\*      \*      \*

## *Easter Prayer*

Shake the foundations of our lives, O Christ,
with your resurrection power to restore and renew.
Where we have seen only boulders, blocking the way to the
future,
give us courage to see
that they will be rolled away—
if we let go of the certainties we have clung to,
if we acknowledge and face our deepest fear of loss
and humbly turn to you in prayer and need.
Give us the hope of Easter, to face with new faith
the personal and worldly cataclysms that
worry and threaten us.
Turn our hearts in prayer each day
to the Holy City, Jerusalem,
to Ramallah and Baghdad,
to all whose lands seethe and sorrow
with ancient hatred and fresh grief.
Hear our prayers for peace,
for a resurrection of sanity,
respect for human dignity,
and reverence for human life
where fear and revenge
now hold sway.

In all the places of darkness and fear, O Christ:
in wounded hearts,
in wounded families,
and in warring countries,
we pray for the earth-shaking
transformation of resurrection
and the rebirth of Easter joy.
Thanks be to God, who has given us the victory
through you, our Risen Christ.  Alleluia!
Amen

\*          \*          \*

## *Eastertide*

Easter greetings! One of the wonderful things about Easter that we often overlook is that it is the longest festival season of the church year—50 days! The lectionary readings throughout Eastertide are faith-tingling stories of Jesus' post-resurrection appearances. One of my favorites is John 20:19-31, the story of Jesus appearing to the disciples and then to Thomas, who hadn't believed their story.

We also missed that first appearance of Jesus after the resurrection. Like Thomas, there are times when we need concrete reassurance of Jesus' continuing presence in our midst. I hope in the pressured, ever-shifting routines and rearrangements of your days this Easter season, the Risen Christ will appear to you in unexpected times and places, in moments of shocking grace, sudden calm, or delicious joy.

## *Eastertide*

Lord, appear to me this Easter season
in ways I don't expect and can't possibly deserve.
When in doubt, I ruminate
on the all-too-obvious troubles that surround me
and the burdens that loom ahead of me,
rather than let go and ask you for help.
Surprise me this Easter, Lord,
into stopping short,
and recognizing that there are Easter possibilities waiting for me
that I haven't imagined,
can't control,
and don't have to manage.
Let me touch your wounded hand,
and feel that the hurts and fears of the past are healed
by the new and redeemed life that is possible now.
With that assurance,
give me the simplicity
to do what is required for this day,
to pray for peace at its beginning and end,
and to trust that you walk ahead of me to Galilee,
preparing my way with love and resurrection light.
Amen

\*          \*          \*

## Spring

Fairest Lord Jesus, ruler of all nature,
We thank you for the blessing of warm sun on our backs and
faces.
Bathed in this balm of spring
gray haired bankers become giddy girls and boys
who sit on park benches
and watch the daffodils shoot toward the sky.
We set down the burdens of war and weariness,
and exult in the touch of warm air on our skin.
Passersby smile.
We thank you for this joy
that stirs from the creature within us,
that bypasses our feverish intellects
to make us laugh and daydream of oceans and lakes and fairways.
We thank you for these hours of healing.
They remind us that your grace and goodness,
like the sun,
are warm, powerful, and sure.
Amen

*       *       *

## Summer

Summer feels as if the kaleidoscope that you have been viewing has suddenly slowed down. There is no less intensity of color. It's just that you can see the shapes more clearly and distinctly. There is still a myriad of stuff and, in some ways, the slower speed intensifies the emotional impact. In our church family we've had baptisms and weddings, new career decisions and impending moves, serious diagnoses, deaths of loved ones. I've had moving and inspiring conversations with some who face the greatest challenges of their lives and are doing so with amazing courage, dignity and grace.

Yet for all its intensity, it's still summer. It's still a time apart—in a way, the Sabbath of our New England calendar—and God still invites us to accept it as a gift and observe it with keen awareness.

## Summer

God, giver of all seasons,
Call me to be fully present to this day.
Let me feel the clamminess
and love the refreshment of a stray breeze
or a window fan.
Let me thank the homeowner I don't know
who years ago planted day lilies that delight me as I drive past.
Let me watch the lightning and fireworks
and have momentarily untroubled memories of childhood.
Let me enjoy seeing vacationing families squeezed into
their minivans,
and remember that no matter what my annoyances,
I'm glad I'm not them.
Help me appreciate the unscheduled moments, even when they
reveal loneliness, grief, or disappointment, that I am too busy to
notice the rest of the year.
Help me treasure the length of days,
the shortness of this season,
and in the midst of it all
find that I am found by you,
and startled,
made aware of summer's bounty
of new prayers and possibilities.
Amen

\*        \*        \*

## *September*

O God,
For whom each day is a new creation,
watch over our mortal beginnings.
Though we may return to the same desks and offices,
our imaginations return in September
to the anxiety of unfamiliar classrooms
and the innocence of unblemished grade books.
Hover palpably, we pray,
'round those we love who start anew,
whether in college or kindergarten.
Be with those of us who yearn and work for different
beginnings,
for new jobs,
new directions,
for new health and hope.
Wherever this fall finds us, give us the gift of your Spirit,
to see in both the tedium and tension of these days,
the possibility for goodness
and the power of love,
as Christ taught us to see and believe.
Amen

\*     \*     \*

# LIFE CELEBRATIONS

---

## *After Worship*

I think of it as Protestant incense:  the lingering scent in the
church sanctuary after Sunday Worship is over. It is a complex
mixture of flowers and candle wax, wood warmed by many
bodies, coffee wafting up from the Community Hour, and most of
all, the sweet, slightly musky scent of many just-showered,
Sunday-dressed church goers. It is deeply evocative of my childhood, and fills the space with a presence that is, as much as any is
to me, a union of human and divine. All those people—praying,
singing, feeling—still seem to inhabit that space that is now empty,
except for their scent and God's silent, living Spirit.

In between Sundays, the faint image of those worshippers
lingers in the sanctuary. As I walk through the church I think of
them, now scattered in their weekday occupations. I pray that as
we all go about our work in the world, we will receive the grace
to celebrate the presence of the Holy Spirit in the day-to-day
miracles, mistakes, and mysteries of life.

It is hard to celebrate, when the uncertainty of life takes
center stage in our consciousness. The uncertainty is always there,
of course, but our minds are remarkably (and I think, mercifully)
adept at planning the future as if it were a sure thing: when and
where we'll take a vacation; where our kids will go to college;
what we're going to do at noon next Friday. In ordinary times, the
presence of the Holy Spirit comes as a welcome "aha" moment in

the midst of things we feel are reasonably under control. In tough times— when we are out of work, facing a really difficult deadline or diagnosis, struggling with emotional illness, or just having a bad day—sensing the presence of the Holy Spirit can be as difficult as defining it. We remember, though, that since the beginning of biblical faith, God's people have called, invoking God's Spirit, and God has responded.

## *After Worship*

Come, Holy Spirit, come,
Spread from the people you have gathered to you in worship
into the lives and communities that need you:
into the pain of aching joints and mental confusion;
the tension of this corporate merger;
the bittersweetness of this graduation;
the space between terror and trust
where I live with my cancer;
into the despair of war and violence;
my fear and worry for my child;
the kite-like emotions of this job search,
which soar and plummet as I try to hold on;
into the cold silent space that seeps into my home
when hearts are closed and distant;
the fatigue and ebbing resilience
of chronic illness;
the piercing pain of a dissolving family;
the tenderness I feel for my aging pet,
the sadness I feel for my aging parent;
into the momentary relief of a soft pillow at night;
the tantalizing warmth of a spring evening;
the joy of laughing with a colleague, a child, a cat,
or a neighbor;
into the intimacy of prayer.

Through your divine alchemy, be present
as a voice on the phone, a loving hug,
a reassuring smile, a quiet sunrise,
an ineffable joy,
and a moment of grace
that wakens us into awareness
that you are with us;
we are not alone.
Amen

\*      \*      \*

\*

## Celebrations

I remembered my axiom about celebrations today. I received the college graduation announcement for a young man I remember vividly as a three-year-old mascot on our Junior Fellowship retreats. I'd already gotten a bunch of high school and college graduation announcements from kids I've known for at least a decade, and sometimes two. Today it finally hit me. My axiom is: we celebrate graduations and other transitions (like weddings) not only because we are happy, but because we are ambivalent. Victory (he did it!) coincides with loss (she won't be here next year) and uncertainty (he's still on the wait list). Having a party, complete with the tension of planning it and cleaning the house, helps us to redirect our thoughts and energy, and get through it all. Spring, for many of us, is a bittersweet time.

For me, opening that graduation announcement was like going down a roller coaster through eighteen years of memories. Pictures flashed by in a blur. There's an album in my head for each child. I can see these kids as shy sixth graders, argumentative seventh graders, bristling or bubbling ninth graders, seniors who flit between triumphant confidence and separation anxiety. If they are now grown up, then I must be older, too. Soon, I will be someone from their past. All these kids, whose personalities and presence have been woven into my life weekly for years are going off to weave their life stories someplace else, with other people. Ouch!

One of my favorite self-help books, called Transitions, by William Bridges, points out the obvious: all beginnings start with endings. So while there is a stab of loss in anticipating these spring galas, and while it is true "things will never be the same," there is also promise. There will be more graduations, weddings, baptisms, and new jobs to celebrate with these glorious young adults; I'll meet moms in the grocery store or after church, and interrogate them about their children's exploits; I'll receive e-mails from all-grown-up-kids who now work in big cities and maybe get home for Christmas. And there are shy sixth graders who are already making a home for themselves in my heart.

So I shake off melancholy and resort to pondering well-worn truths. Each day is a precious gift. We never have any more than today. And today, no matter how tense or lousy or routine it is, I can make a difference in someone's life. I resolve to listen, really listen, to my son's after school or bedtime monologue, remembering that in a blink of an eye, he'll be grown.

## Celebrations

Thank you, God, for the privilege of touching lives,
of knowing and being known.
Thank you for the faces, voices, and experiences
I hold dear in memory.
Thank you for this day;
give me grace to live it fully.
Help me catch hold of my sadness
over the passing of time,
examine it,
and then let it go—
like a moth I catch and shoo from a bright kitchen door
on a summer night.
Remind me to take just a moment longer
to appreciate someone today
who might have passed through my life unnoticed.
Remind me to listen,
really listen
to someone I think I know all too well.
Help me to find meaning in the routine
and surprise in the predictable;
for I know that your Spirit is alive and untamed,
able to breathe new life into the most ordinary times and places.

Help me accept the loss
that comes even with good change,
trusting that your will for me,
for those I love,
and for your human family
is deepening joy and wisdom and communion with you,
through the One who gave his life
so that we might have life abundant and life eternal.
Amen

\*        \*        \*

## Fiftieth Birthday I

Fifty thanks and blessings, O God,
for the gift of our fifty-year-old friend!
He makes fifty seem young—
his energy seems like an endless spring.

He is even more precious to us now
than when he was young,
because we've shared so many things—
good, bad, and ridiculous—
which we wouldn't trade for any fountain of youth.
We pray for long life,
new adventures,
good health and sight,
professional recognition,
increasing freedom,
meaningful work,
nourishing leisure,
communion with you,
and affection and laughter
with a wealth of friends and loved ones
for this beloved half centenarian
and special child of God.
Amen!

\*          \*          \*

## Fiftieth Birthday II

If this is a milestone, O God,
someone forgot to tell my mirror.
I look the same as I did yesterday,
though certainly not the same as I did
ten years ago.
And that's the comparison that's got my attention.

Surely, at fifty, I have crossed the midpoint
of my life's journey,
and I'm not sure how I feel about it.
There are things I'm proud of,
people I love,
accomplishments logged in.
But there's an irritating tickle
in the back of my brain
that keeps me coughing up pesky thoughts:
Is this it?  Is this the peak?
I feel unfinished, and not all that grown up.
Will people still hire me?
Do I still have the energy I had,
or will folks pay for the wisdom that has replaced some of it?
Be with me, O God,
and help me celebrate this momentous divide
between my first half century and my second.

Replace my feelings of being old,
with a feeling of being a newly minted half-dollar,
more valuable than a quarter or a dime,
a whole lot handier than 50 pennies,
and held precious and safe in your hand,
ready to be used for something
new and special that's yet to come.
Amen

\*          \*          \*

## Wedding

There must be some mistake, God.
A wedding is a celebration, right?
Then why do I feel so anxious, so ambivalent,
so overwhelmed with the details
and frayed around the edges?
As much as we have looked forward to this day
there's something about its coming that is sudden and wrenching,
stirring up memories and feelings
about other beginnings and endings, ceremonies and changes
we didn't invite to this event.
Steady me, God. Steady all of us—
the relatives who will all bring their histories
to the family potluck,
the bride and groom who are afraid and happy,
the parent who is excited and whose heart is about to burst
with memory and pride.
Remind us, as we jostle and negotiate with each other,
that you are right here with us.
Your loving presence fills the family photos,
and your quiet peace invades our storming emotions.
Remind us when that precious covenant is made,
it is you who make it,
who call us all into a new day of faithful service
and loving companionship
through Christ, our Lord.
Amen

*     *     *

# SEPTEMBER 11th

*Sunday, September 16, 2001*

Loving God,
who sustains us in sorrow and restores us to joy,
how good it is to be together in your house.
Here, among our friends in Christ,
joined in common loss and common hope,
stirred to tears by hymns of praise,
we are free to release the burdens of the week;
able to trust that your infinite strength and limitless love
can safely hold whatever we feel, whatever we fear,
whatever befalls us now, and in the future.
We thank you for all that is most precious to us:
the love of family and friends,
the support of community,
the greatness of this nation, its moral character revealed
as fully in its restraint and self-reflection,
as in its resiliency and resolve.

We thank you for the people of all races and religions,
all shades of personal and political belief,
who live together in peace and in mutual respect in our land.
Continue, we pray, to pour upon all people of this land
your spirit of reconciliation and peace,
even as we unite to face a threat

we fear and do not understand.
Give us grace in all the days ahead,
as our hearts and minds ricochet
between trauma and blessed tedium,
the extraordinary and oh-so-welcome ordinary,
to trust in your unfailing care
and to hope in your healing will for all your children.
For all your people, especially for those among us who mourn
most deeply, O God, bring comfort and restoration.
In your time, kindle anew the ashes of joy,
and grant us your peace,
which passes all understanding,
today and always,
through our Lord, Jesus Christ.
Amen

\*      \*      \*

## Monday, September 17, 2001

God of all creation,
I never before thought of going to work
as a statement of faith.
But here we are, my colleagues and I
and others throughout this land,
newly called to the work we do
in a world that is both familiar and unrecognizable.
Bless us this day as we go about our jobs.
Help us focus on doing our work
as well and as nobly as we know how.
Remind us
that the ultimate end of building our business
and strengthening the economy
is to create resources to care for people
here, and across the globe.
Remind us, in the end, that ensuring justice
and sharing by all, so there is scarcity for none,
is the ultimate weapon against hatred;
and that our work today is connected to that great work.
In the inevitable moments of sadness and confusion,
remind us to turn to you,
and to one another
with a new caring, a recognition, born of this tragedy,
that we work not just with colleagues or competitors,
but with our brothers and sisters.
Amen

*       *       *

## Tuesday, September 25, 2001

There are moments, O God,
when I am still so sad.
Then there are moments when I become mercifully absorbed
in the stuff of my life,
and I feel a little guilty for it.
There are moments when I am angry
and don't know whether there is more fear or fury in my gut.
There are moments when I laugh and forget,
and I feel such blessed relief.
Accept all of these feelings, O God,
as I struggle toward healing,
and help me to accept them, too.
In your time,
heal these fresh wounds of my heart and of our nation.
Give us together renewed strength
and new understanding
to become healers of the wounds
that devastate so many children in our global human family.
Help me to work, and love, and pray today
with an intense gratitude
for the gifts of life,
and for the opportunity to use them in your service.
Amen

\*      \*      \*

# INDEX